ABOUT ISLAND PRESS

Island Press, a nonprofit organization, publishes, markets, and distributes the most advanced thinking on the conservation of our natural resources—books about soil, land, water, forests, wildlife, and hazardous and toxic wastes. These books are practical tools used by public officials, business and industry leaders, natural resource managers, and concerned citizens working to solve both local and global resource problems.

Founded in 1978, Island Press reorganized in 1984 to meet the increasing demand for substantive books on all resource-related issues. Island Press publishes and distributes under its own imprint and offers these services to other nonprofit organizations.

Support for Island Press is provided by Apple Computers, Inc., Mary Reynolds Babcock Foundation, Geraldine R. Dodge Foundation, The Educational Foundation of America, The Charles Engelhard Foundation, The Ford Foundation, Glen Eagles Foundation, The George Gund Foundation, The William and Flora Hewlett Foundation, The Joyce Foundation, The J. M. Kaplan Fund, The John D. and Catherine T. MacArthur Foundation, The Andrew W. Mellon Foundation, The Joyce Mertz-Gilmore Foundation, The New-Land Foundation, The Jessie Smith Noyes Foundation, The J. N. Pew, Jr., Charitable Trust, Alida Rockefeller, The Rockefeller Brothers Fund, The Florence and John Schumann Foundation, The Tides Foundation, and individual donors.

COASTAL ALERT

COASTAL ALERT

Ecosystems, Energy, and Offshore Oil Drilling

Dwight Holing

*Natural Resources Defense Council
and the
Central Coast Regional Studies Program*

*FOREWORD BY TED DANSON
American Oceans Campaign*

ISLAND PRESS

Washington, D.C. • *Covelo, California*

Grateful acknowledgment is made to the following for permission
to reprint material appearing in Appendix 3:

The Orlando Sentinel, for "Why We Don't Want Offshore Oil
Drilling," February 11, 1990.

Carteret County News, for "Public Hearings Can Stop Mobil,"
January 3, 1989, which appears under the heading Model Press
Advisory.

Rachel Heyman, for "Letter to the Editor: Cost of
Drilling," *San Francisco Chronicle,* March 7, 1990.

Ocean Sanctuary Coordinating Committee of Mendocino,
California, for "Letter to the Editor: Ocean Sanctuary,"
San Francisco Chronicle, January 25, 1990.

Library of Congress Cataloging-in-Publication Data

Holing, Dwight. Coastal alert: ecosystems, energy, and
offshore oil drilling / Dwight Holing.
p. cm. — (Island Press critical issues series: #2)
Includes bibliographical references.
ISBN 1-55963-050-7 (paper)
1. Oil well drilling, Submarine—Environmental aspects—
United States. 2. Energy development—Decision
making—Citizen participation. I. Title. II. Series

TD195.P4H64 1990   90-41293
333.8'23214—dc20   CIP

Printed on recycled, acid-free paper
Manufactured in the United States of America
10 9 8 7 6 5 4 3 2

The sea does not belong to despots.

—Jules Verne

Roll on, thou deep and dark blue ocean—roll!
Ten thousand fleets sweep over thee in vain;
Man marks the earth with ruin—his control
Stops with the shore.

—Lord Byron

Contents

Acknowledgments

This handbook, a cooperative venture undertaken by NRDC and funded by the Central Coast Regional Studies Program, is concrete evidence of what can be accomplished when concerned citizens, professional environmentalists, and local government officials unite to achieve a single goal.

Special credit goes to Ann Notthoff, NRDC Senior Project Planner, and Warner Chabot, Central Coast Regional Studies Program Regional Coordinator, who coordinated the entire project. This book would not have been possible without the invaluable contributions made by Richard Charter, Local Government Coordinating Program Executive Director, and Johanna Wald and Lisa Speer, NRDC Senior Attorney and Scientist. Thanks also go to Tyler Johnson, Lesley Estes, and Eliza Brown for their assistance, to Gretchen Treuting for design, and to Hazel Westney for word processing.

The Natural Resources Defense Council (NRDC) is a private nonprofit environmental protection organization founded in 1970. With principal offices in New York, Washington, D.C., San Francisco, and Los Angeles, NRDC's staff of lawyers, scientists and resource specialists addresses a range of critical environmental problems in the United States and worldwide. NRDC is supported by its more than 130,000 members and contributors, over 90,000 of whom reside in coastal states.

The Central Coast Regional Studies Program is a cooperative effort of six California coastal counties, each represented by a county supervisor. The participating counties are: Sonoma, represented by Ernie Carpenter; Marin, by Gary Giacomini; San Francisco, by Angela Alioto; San Mateo, by Anna Eshoo; Santa Cruz, by Gary Patton, and Monterey, by Marc del Piero. The regional program studies the impacts of proposed offshore oil drilling along California's Central Coast and evaluates and comments on industry and federal documents. The program emphasizes public education and involvement in the federal decision process through workshops and publication of newsletters, fact sheets, and citizen guides.

Cover photo by Bob Sollen

Foreword

I grew up in Arizona but have lived most of my adult life on the westernmost edge of the continent, the Pacific lapping at my door. The ocean—its beauty, mystery, power, and grace—plays upon all of my senses: the briny smell, the cracking sound of surf, the sting of spindrift, the taste of salt, the sun sparkling on the water. It also touches something beyond the sensory, something deep below the surface of my consciousness: that part of me—that part of all of us—that can be traced back to the day life first awoke in the sea 3.5 billion years ago.

I'm not exactly sure why the ocean affects me the way it does, but I do know this: the ocean's well-being is key to our survival. Not only did the sea give birth to us, but it continues to sustain us. The ocean covers more than three-fifths of the globe. It controls our weather, gives us rain, supplies us with food, and provides us with 70 percent of our oxygen. Yet for all its vastness, its overwhelming power, the ocean is extremely fragile and vulnerable to rapid, irrevocable degradation by man.

A few years ago I took my two daughters to the beach for a swim. A "Keep Out" sign was posted near the water. The fine print warned us that the ocean was polluted and unsafe for swimming. My daughters asked me how something as big as the Pacific could get so dirty. I didn't know what to tell them, but I became determined to find the answer. What I learned frightened and angered me as a parent and as a citizen. I discovered that ours wasn't the only beach that was suffering; beaches everywhere have become polluted. Toxic runoff, untreated sewage, and industrial wastes are contaminating all the oceans. One of the worst offenders and biggest threats of all, I learned, is oil production.

To put it simply, oil and water don't mix. The black tide from the *Exxon Valdez* surely proved that. So did the multiple spills that occurred within the following year in Arthur Kill, New York, and off Texas, New England, and Huntington Beach, California. Yet these lessons appear to have been lost on the members of our own federal government who would allow oil companies to drill in the waters off our nation's beaches and shoreline. Many of these areas are comparable to our finest national parks. Some hold more wildlife than Yellowstone, others more geological grandeur than the Grand Canyon. Nevertheless, they are being considered for oil drilling—a destiny few of us would contemplate were Yosemite at stake.

Now, I know a thing or two about comedy, but this is no joke. The government is deadly serious about leasing more of our coastal waters to oil companies, despite the fact that drilling promises more oil spills, more air pollution, and more toxic wastes being dumped into the sea.

We need to prevent that from happening in order to protect America's oceans and, ultimately, ourselves. There are many things we can do as individual citizens and as groups. That is why I founded the American Oceans Campaign—to help people learn how to make a difference and to remind us of what can happen if we don't. We need to get involved in the political process at both the local and national levels if we are to solve the problem posed by the government's plans for offshore oil drilling.

This book has the information we need to do just that. I urge you to read it. It has been prepared by the Natural Resources Defense Council, a national organization that has a solid record of research and advocacy on behalf of the environment. It not only identifies the dangers associated with oil drilling, but also teaches us what we as citizens can do to save our oceans and beaches. It also provides safe and practical alternatives to drilling so we can meet our national energy needs without sacrificing our environment.

It is up to us to protect our oceans. We must act now. If we don't, we'll have a lot of explaining to do to our children and our children's children.

Ted Danson, President
American Oceans Campaign

Introduction

SHIFTING CURRENTS

The huge cost of our dependence on fossil fuels was vividly illustrated on March 24, 1989, when the American tanker *Exxon Valdez* floundered on Bligh Reef, spilling nearly 11 million gallons of Alaskan crude oil into the pristine waters of Prince William Sound. The slick coated over 1,200 miles of scenic coastline, clogging countless bays and inlets, as well as the stomachs, fur, and feathers of thousands of sea otters, sea lions, seabirds, and fish, not to mention bears and eagles that ingested the oily remains of dead animals washed up onshore and deer that browsed along the contaminated shoreline.

Wildlife weren't the only victims of this terrible accident. So were thousands of Native Alaskans and workers dependent upon subsistence and commercial fishing and tourism. Both industries came crashing to a halt. And despite more than $2 billion and months of work, efforts to clean the mess up failed miserably. It will be years, even decades, before the most visible signs of this human-generated catastrophe can be erased. And there is no guarantee that the area's ecology will ever fully recover. There is grim and disturbing evidence that oil pollution is chronic and its impacts are irreversible.

The *Exxon Valdez* disaster demonstrates just how defenseless we are when it comes to protecting our treasured coastline from the impacts of oil spills. Even more alarming, the tanker could have just as easily run aground off the coast of California or along the Atlantic shore or in the Florida Keys. The fact is, no stretch of the nation's coast is free from the risk of an oil spill of this magnitude. Our vulnerability is not restricted solely to the transportation of oil, either. Every aspect of the fossil fuel cycle has its dangers.

This is especially true when it comes to offshore oil drilling. The process of extracting energy from our coastal waters poses an immediate threat to the marine environment, not to mention to our way of life onshore. Each step of offshore development, from drilling to transport to processing, exposes land, air, and water to a host of dangerous pollutants. Toxic wastes and air pollutants are just a few of the unhealthful by-products. Offshore drilling also means onshore industrialization and considerable economic conflict with existing economies. The destructive legacy of offshore drilling will be with us long after the final drop of oil is drained and consumed.

The dangers associated with offshore oil drilling have stirred considerable public debate over the federal government's plans to lease additional areas of the nation's coast to the oil industry. On June 26, 1990, as a result of enormous political pressure, President George Bush announced his intention to delay drilling plans until the year 2000 in six coastal areas, including California, the Florida Keys, and New England's Georges Bank, while further environmental studies are conducted.

While the decision affords important protection for certain geographical areas, it does not end the threat from offshore oil and gas drilling; it simply postpones it in those areas. The presidential delay is not permanent and, because it is an administrative action, rather than an act of Congress, it can be revoked at will. The delay cannot bind future presidents. Nor does it cover many of the nation's environmentally sensitive coastal areas, including much of the Eastern Seaboard, Northern Florida, and Alaska. These areas contain much more than energy resources. Alaska's Bristol Bay, for example, is a wildlife wonderland, home to more than a dozen species of marine mammals and roughly two million seabirds. The Atlantic's Barrier Islands support a multi-million dollar tourist economy.

The environmental risk to these areas from drilling is immense. According to official government estimates, additional offshore drilling will likely cause twenty-two to forty-six major oil spills—but oil spills aren't the only environmental danger. Offshore oil development will also seriously degrade water quality. Thousands of tons of wastes, some of them toxic, are dumped into the ocean each time a well is drilled, potentially contaminating fish and other marine life. Additional offshore platforms and their associated machinery will fill the skies with even more pollutants, further increasing the levels of smog and acid rain and global warming. The construction of onshore support facilities will alter the face of the nation's already beleaguered coastline. Industrial development brings industrial pollution to undeveloped areas and adds a great burden to already heavily developed areas. Noise from aircraft and boat traffic will disrupt the natural behavior of some sensitive species. Dredging for pipelines will destroy vital wetlands, those important ecosystems that serve as the nation's kidneys by filtering some types of pollutants through natural action.

The federal government has long maintained that all these costs to the environment are worth it in order to increase America's supply of oil and end our dependence on foreign oil. But there is little basis for that reasoning. Only 5.5 billion barrels of oil equivalent are estimated to

Photo by Marion Stirrup

The 1989 Exxon Valdez *oil spill ignited a national debate over the environmental risks associated with oil development.*

underlie the nation's outer continental shelf (OCS), excluding that contained in the central and western Gulf of Mexico. This represents only 323 days' worth of energy at 17 million barrels per day, the current rate of consumption. Offshore oil won't reduce our dependence on foreign oil. Total U.S. domestic reserves represent only a small fraction of the world's petroleum reserves, yet we consume 25 percent of the world's fossil fuel. As long as we use oil to fuel our nation, we will continue to rely on foreign sources.

Actually there is a much less expensive and much more environmentally prudent way to add to the nation's energy supplies than drilling offshore. The technology exists today to make automobiles, buildings, and factories that use half as much energy as they do now. By raising automobile gas mileage standards, weatherizing houses and other buildings, expanding mass transit, and using more-energy-efficient light bulbs, windows, and appliances, we can save the equivalent of 45 billion barrels of oil by the year 2020. This "conservation oil field" makes the deposits underlying the OCS pale in comparison.

A barrel of oil produced from savings contributes just as much to our national energy supply as a barrel of oil squeezed from the ground. Furthermore, efficiency will keep producing energy indefinitely, while the average offshore oil well will run dry in ten to twenty years. An efficient furnace purchased in 1995 will still be saving energy in 2014. A house insulated in 1990 will still be saving oil in the year 2050. Investments in improved energy efficiency will be far more cost effective than investments in offshore oil or electricity from new power plants. Energy efficiency will also help reduce marine pollution and onshore industrialization associated with offshore oil development, not to mention urban air pollution, acid rain, and global warming.

We must insist that the government embrace energy efficiency as our national energy policy rather than allow oil companies to plunder our fragile and limited offshore natural resources. Each of us needs to speak out in support of national energy reform. We need to become active participants in the nationwide movement to protect our coasts by halting new offshore oil drilling plans in sensitive areas. To do that, we need to participate in the lease sale process—the bureaucratic procedure that governs OCS development activities.

The nation's federal offshore energy resources are managed by the U.S. Department of the Interior (DOI). The Secretary of the Interior

Photo by Bob Sollen

Oil from the drilling platforms that line California's Santa Barbara Channel could easily reach shore in the event of an accident.

develops a leasing schedule of the OCS that he determines will best meet national energy needs, a so-called five-year program. At the same time, the secretary is required by law to balance drilling plans with environmental and regional onshore socioeconomic concerns. This gives the public the opportunity to influence the outcome of the secretary's programs.

It is vital that citizens speak out on behalf of the environment and local concerns during these opportunities, because the government's leasing program is tipped heavily in favor of drilling. To begin with, the methods that the DOI employs to assess the environmental impacts of proposed lease sales are based on inadequate scientific information. That is the conclusion of a 1989 study conducted by the National Academy of Sciences' prestigious National Research Council.

The economic formula used for leasing is inherently flawed as well. Lease sales are commonly held when oil prices are low. This results in low lease prices, often as little as $25 per acre. The oil companies then sell the oil back to the public when prices are high. The result is billions of dollars of profits for the oil companies made at our expense and from our own publicly owned natural resources.

Our challenge is to stop drilling before the lease sale process even begins, because once leases are granted, they are never canceled. Not only has the DOI never canceled a lease, it has never denied an OCS development and production plan submitted by an oil company. The best way to protect our coasts is to place a permanent ban on offshore oil drilling in environmentally sensitive areas. Such a bill has already been introduced in Congress. It is called the Ocean Protection Act of 1990. Endorsed by a bipartisan coalition of coastal state congressional representatives, the act would create a permanent ocean sanctuary. It needs your support.

Until the Ocean Protection Act is enacted in law, we need to keep active in the lease sale process. Citizen involvement is still an effective means of shaping the outcome of the federal government's plans for the OCS. Grass-roots groups such as those in California have used public participation opportunities during the lease sale process successfully to challenge previous government plans. Combined with lawsuits and congressional intervention, citizen action has effectively limited the spread of drilling off California and other areas of the nation's coast. President Bush's June 1990 call for a ten-year delay for drilling off California is proof positive that citizen action works.

This primer and handbook was written to provide you with an understanding of offshore oil production and the serious environmental consequences it poses. It was prepared by the Natural Resources Defense Council with funds provided by the Central Coast Regional Studies Program, a coalition of six California local governments that believes that an informed citizenry can be effective in changing federal policies and priorities.

The book begins with an explanation of how the government is selling our coast to big oil, and provides a step-by-step guide to how the lease sale process works so that you can identify opportunities for public participation. Next, the book describes how offshore drilling affects the environment as well as our quality of life onshore. An explanation is given in clear, easy-to-grasp terms on how oil and gas are extracted from coastal waters. To demonstrate how citizen action can be effective, the California experience is chronicled as a case study and role model. Finally, the book identifies the alternatives to offshore drilling and makes recommendations for national energy policy reform and long-lasting ocean protection.

As citizens, we have a responsibility to make sure that the government pursues an energy policy that neither produces a polluting source of energy nor contributes to a delay in the necessary and inevitable shift toward clean energy resources.

America's coast belongs to all of us. We can determine its future. By becoming informed, by becoming involved, we can protect our coast now and for generations to come.

1 DOI, BIG OIL, AND YOU

How the Government Is Selling Our Coast to Big Oil

North America does not end at the beach. Beyond where waves lap at sand and rock, the continent ducks beneath the ocean and slopes gently toward the horizon for miles and miles. Scientists call this watery edge of the mainland the outer continental shelf, or OCS. It is one of nature's true treasure troves, replete with a bounty of biological resources and resplendent in natural beauty and wonder. The OCS also contains scattered deposits of oil and gas trapped beneath the sea bottom. Their presence has triggered a tremendous conflict between developing them and protecting the coast's natural resources.

Since 1953, the government has been auctioning huge tracts of the publicly owned OCS to oil companies. The government agency in charge of scheduling and overseeing these sales is the Department of the Interior (DOI). Under the Outer Continental Shelf Lands Act of 1953 as amended (OCSLA), the Secretary of the Interior is charged with preparing and implementing so-called five-year programs. The secretary judges what the nation's energy requirements will be for a five-year period, then selects undersea areas and develops a schedule to lease them to oil companies in order to help fulfill those needs. At the same time, he must balance these plans with environmental protection measures and take into consideration the concerns of local governments.

The actual leasing is managed by the Minerals Management Service (MMS), an agency within the Interior Department. The MMS invites oil companies to bid against each other for the rights to specified nine-mile-square tracts in a process called a lease sale. The highest bidder wins. The government has held 100 sales between 1954 and 1988 and leased 53.27 million acres, an area as large as the entire state of Florida. Nearly 28,000 wells have been drilled on the OCS so far.

Huge areas of the nation's coast can be included in a five-year program. The "Mid-1987 to Mid-1992 Five-Year Program," for instance, proposed thirty-eight lease sales covering more than 700 million acres, over half of the entire OCS. That's an area nearly twice the size of Alaska. The program was engineered by former Secretary of the Interior Donald Hodel, who modeled it after a plan designed by his predecessor, James Watt. During his tenure, Watt proposed leasing virtually all of the nation's coastal waters. The areas originally targeted by the 1987-92 plan include the waters and the wildlife, marine resources, and scenic splendor that go with them off Alaska, Washington, Oregon, California, Texas, Louisiana, Mississippi, Alabama, Florida, Georgia, South Carolina, North Carolina, Virginia, Maryland, Delaware, Pennsylvania, New Jersey, New York, Connecticut, Rhode Island, Massachusetts, New Hampshire, and Maine.

What Is at Stake

The nation's OCS is divided into twenty-six planning areas: four along the East Coast (North, Mid-, and South Atlantic, and Straits of Florida), three in the Gulf of Mexico (Eastern, Central, and Western), four along the West Coast (Southern, Central, and Northern California, and Washington-Oregon), and fifteen in Alaska (Cook Inlet, Shumagin, North Aleutian Basin, St. George Basin, Navarin Basin, Norton Basin, Hope Basin, Chukchi Sea, Beaufort Sea, Gulf of Alaska, Kodiak, Aleutian Arc, Bowers Basin, Aleutian Basin, and St. Matthew Hall).

These planning areas support a number of non-energy-related coastal and marine industries, including tourism and commercial fishing. The myriad environmental consequences that accompany offshore de-

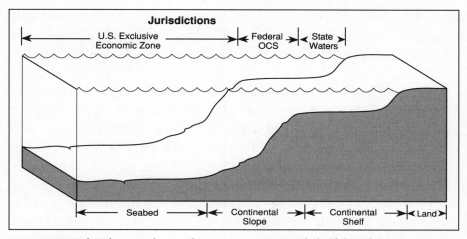

FIGURE 1 *Federal control over the outer continental shelf (OCS) begins three miles from shore.*
Source: Central Coast Regional Studies Program

velopment jeopardize the resources these activities depend upon.

The North Atlantic planning area, for instance, is home to Georges Bank, a remarkable fishery that has been a mainstay of the New England fishing industry for over three hundred years. It supports over forty thousand jobs and sustains a fishing industry worth approximately $1.5 billion annually. Georges Bank's unique circular current, shallow depth, and unusual turbulence combine to make it one of the most productive fisheries anywhere in the world. The area's submarine canyons and other undersea lands provide vital habitats for a variety of commercial seafood species, including tilefish, swordfish, tuna, red hake, and lobster.

The Mid-Atlantic planning area to the south also supports a robust commercial fishery, one worth more than $200 million annually. It is rich in biological resources, including a diverse array of fish, birds, and marine mammals, several of which are considered endangered. The coastal area here lies within the Atlantic Flyway. Over three million migratory waterfowl travel this flyway annually, with more than two-thirds of these birds wintering in the coastal wetlands of the mid-Atlantic states. Cape May County, New Jersey, is one of the most important regions in the Western Hemisphere for migratory shorebirds. At least three seabirds that breed here are listed as endangered or threatened: the least tern, roseate tern, and black skimmer. Some thirty species of whales swim offshore. Six are endangered, including the northern right whale. No more than three hundred such whales are thought to exist. The thousand-mile shoreline from Cape Cod to Cape Hatteras is composed predominantly of sandy beaches and barrier islands. It attracts millions of tourists annually.

The South Atlantic region off the Carolinas, Georgia, and northern Florida supports a vital tourist economy as well. Visitors are drawn by the area's abundance of national and state parks, wildlife refuges, and national seashores that line the coasts in all four states. Shorebirds, wading birds, and waterfowl depend on its coastal and nearshore areas. The waters off Cape Hatteras and along the western edge of the Gulf Stream are important feeding areas for several unusual bird species, including the Bermuda petrel and brown pelican, both of which are on the federal list of endangered species. The region supports several other threatened or endangered species, including bald eagles, wood storks, American alligators, Atlantic marsh snakes, short-nosed sturgeons, and three endangered and two threatened species of sea turtles.

The Straits of Florida planning area is one of the nation's coastal crown jewels. It encompasses extraordinarily sensitive and highly productive areas of seagrass beds, mangrove swamps, forested wetlands, coastal marshes, estuarine areas, and barrier islands, as well as the largest coral reef system on the North American continent. In addition, the region supports many endangered species, including five species of whales, four species of sea turtles, and the manatee. The southwest Florida shelf lies adjacent to Everglades National Park, the Florida Keys, two national marine sanctuaries, two national wildlife sanctuaries, a national natural landmark, two national wilderness areas, and an aquatic preserve. Over one million out-of-state tourists travel to the Keys each year. They spend millions of dollars on hotels, food, rental of diving equipment, and other services.

Tourism also plays a key role in all three California planning areas. In 1988, tourists spent $27 billion in California's coastal counties, accounting for 86 percent of the state's total tourism revenue.

Southern California's sandy, sun-kissed beaches attract visitors from all over the world. Both recreational and commercial fishing industries thrive here. The region boasts a plethora of wildlife, including several endangered species.

The Central California region contains the world's greatest diversity

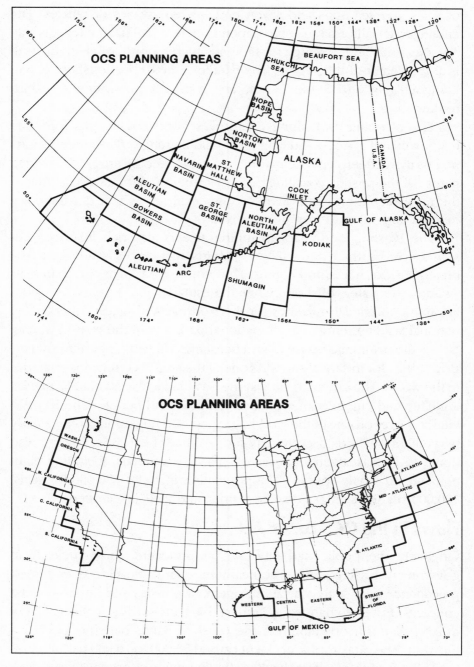

FIGURE 2 *The Department of the Interior has divided the nation's OCS into twenty-six planning areas.*

Source: Minerals Management Service

of seals and sea lions and seven endangered species of whales. The endangered California sea otter depends on this vital habitat for survival. Año Nuevo Island, a refuge for the endangered northern elephant seal, is at the center of this region. The Farallon Islands, just offshore of San Francisco's fabled Golden Gate, are considered a premier seabird rookery.

The planning area along California's north coast abuts forty-one major wetland systems and a national wildlife refuge. The area supports no less than fifteen separate marine mammal breeding areas. The rugged nature of the pristine coastline makes Northern California's coast one of the most scenic on earth. Many of the small towns that dot the coast depend largely on tourism for survival.

The Washington-Oregon planning area is also rich in marine resources. More than one million seabirds rely on its sandy beaches, offshore rocks, inlets, and islands. Thirty-three types of marine mammals swim in the waters offshore, while the estuaries and wetlands onshore are home to critical nurseries for the Northwest's biggest fisheries. Six national wildlife refuges and a national park adjoin the coastal waters.

All the planning areas in Alaska boast incredible biological resources. Bristol Bay, for instance, supports one of the largest commercial fisheries in the world. The salmon fishery alone is valued in excess of $250 million annually and employs an estimated ten thousand people. The Bay is a vital stopover on one of the world's greatest bird migration routes. Nearly two million seabirds occupy sixty-four colonies here. Bristol Bay is also home to at least twenty species of marine mammals, including eight endangered whale species. The population includes 870,000 fur seals, 100,000 sea lions, 50,000 Pacific walrus, and 20,000 sea otters.

Flaws in the OCS Lands Act

Originally the public had little say in protecting these areas from government leasing plans. The headlong rush to develop energy took precedence over state coastal management policies and environmental concerns. But that changed in January 1969 after a Union Oil Company drilling platform operating off the coast of Santa Barbara suffered a blowout. The catastrophic accident caused 50,000 to 70,000 barrels of oil to gush out of the well unchecked, fouling miles of beaches with black ooze and seriously harming the coastal ecology of the region. Public reaction to the spill was visceral and vocal. Virtually overnight citizen groups organized and began calling for the government to place stricter regulations on offshore drilling. People living up and down the California coast demanded a say in how the Department of the Interior managed the coastal waters next to where they lived. Residents in other coastal states soon echoed the same demands.

The government responded by amending the OCS Lands Act in 1978. Key among the changes were provisions that gave citizens and local and state governments somewhat more opportunity to participate in OCS policy and planning decisions. As a result, the lease sale process was expanded to include public hearings in which citizens could nominate areas that should or should not be leased, review and comment on environmental impact statements, and make specific recommendations concerning the government's entire five-year program. The amendments to OCSLA also gave the state more input. The DOI and MMS were required to consult with state agencies regarding leasing plans, and the affected state's governor was given the opportunity to make an official recommendation.

Despite these changes, the lease sale system—the bureaucratic process that governs OCS development activities—remains flawed. A 1989 study conducted by the National Academy of Sciences, which was commissioned by the White House to review the Outer Continental Shelf Environmental Studies Program, concluded that the DOI has been proceeding with oil drilling leases despite insufficient scientific information regarding environmental and socioeconomic impacts. The report found the DOI's information so imperfect as to provide an inadequate basis for a decision to proceed with leasing, the first step in the oil exploration process.

Of underlying concern to the report's authors is the fact that there is no separation of leasing from development and production during the lease sale process. Studies sponsored by the government under the Environmental Studies Program, like the assessments found in the DOI's environmental impact statements, have focused almost entirely on the lease sale stage. Two fundamental problems result from this practice. First, the exact location of oil is unknown at the prelease stage. Consequently, it is impossible to identify the exact location of future facilities and to accurately predict specific environmental impacts of development. This also makes it difficult to balance the national benefits of production against the environmental risks. Second, by the time producing reservoirs are identified, the oil companies typically have committed enormous amounts of money to the lease. The DOI has never canceled a lease, although it has authority to do so. So a decision to lease is tantamount to a decision to develop and produce, provided that the oil company wants to drill.

In spite of provisions for further analysis and review at later stages in lease sale planning, many local, state, and federal government officials doubt that adequate analysis will be performed and that decision alternatives will be preserved through the process. Members of the NAS committee conducting the study say they were told by MMS officials that out of the hundreds of actual OCS development plans submitted by oil companies since 1978, none has ever been denied by the DOI.

Throughout the history of OCS development, the Department of the Interior has rarely deferred sensitive ecological areas from lease sales except for areas of minimal oil industry interest. When deferrals are made or buffer zones around important habitats are created, they are usually inadequate to provide real protection from oil spills and toxic discharges.

As was so tragically demonstrated by the *Exxon Valdez* accident, response, containment, and cleanup are slow and technologically inadequate when oil spills do occur. Nevertheless, lease sale stipulations generally fail to require measures that will reduce the potential of oil spills and increase spill response.

Adequate air pollution controls are not required by Interior officials, either. Offshore standards are frequently less rigorous than onshore standards. This is most vividly illustrated in areas such as Southern California, which is already suffering under the veil of the most polluted air in the nation. Usually, no meaningful effort is made to protect vital fisheries, either by deferring specific tracts or by imposing lease stipulations that will effectively minimize conflicts.

The single most important failure of current offshore development policies is the absence of a comprehensive, well-rationalized "least cost" national energy plan that would require Interior to compare the costs and benefits of drilling with alternative energy programs. Valuable resources are being placed at significant risk by virtue of a lack of long-term planning and little, if any, consideration of alternatives.

Photo by Chris Calwell

The nation's publicly owned offshore lands are one of our greatest treasures.

The Interior Department expects the public to accept the risks of such damaging consequences despite overwhelming evidence that the oil reserves off the nation's coasts are dwarfed by potential "energy reserves" from efficiency policies ignored by the federal government. Our current reliance on unfettered fossil fuel consumption has created environmental consequences of immense proportion—acid rain and global warming. Finally, fears regarding the implications of importing foreign oil have traditionally been overstated by the government. The past and current administrations have done little to reduce imports. Nor has enough been done to increase energy efficiency. As a result, the nation's current national energy policy, which calls for increasing the rate of depleting America's oil reserves through offshore drilling, does not help secure our national energy security.

Participating in the Process

The lease sale process has enormous political and ecological implications. It is a complex and lengthy bureaucratic undertaking that takes, on average, two years to complete. Leasing involves a series of labyrinthine steps, but citizens can pressure the DOI to negotiate and compromise. Intense and ongoing dialogue between private citizens, public interest groups, state and local government, the DOI, the MMS, and the oil industry can surround virtually every stage of the process.

The MMS plays a central role in these negotiations and makes ultimate decisions, since it defines the steps in the decision process, the subject matter and scope of decisions, and the timetable for particular lease sales. State and local governments also have a lead role in the negotiation process. They have in many instances become the policy protagonists for environmental and socioeconomic issues. The public has an important part to play as well. Citizens influence the negotiations by defining public attitudes and determining the value placed on ocean and coastal resources affected by oil drilling.

The entire lease sale process is outlined step by step in Appendix A and briefly explained below. Several steps are expressly keyed to direct public participation. The first is the "Call for Information." The MMS asks the oil industry and the public to nominate areas they want to drill. The public may suggest areas that should not be drilled. This is called a negative nomination. You can submit a nomination or negative nomination for a portion or all of the coast. Your nomination can include personal observations and values.

The Call is also sent directly to the governor of each affected state. The governor is asked to identify issues and topics of concern that should be considered in the development of the initial leasing proposal. Because the governor solicits input from state and local officials, this is a good opportunity for citizen involvement. You can ask your local representatives to represent your views and concerns on potential environmental impacts and conflicts. Speaking out at this juncture can help influence your governor's official comments.

Afterward comes "Area Identification/Environmental Impact Statement Scoping." The MMS identifies the specific area to be studied in the environmental impact statement and asks for input on the issues it should address. Once again, you can formally comment on various issues as well as propose alternatives and mitigation measures. This is another stage at which local and state government officials can respond, so make sure your representatives reflect your viewpoint.

A draft environmental impact statement is released and one or more public hearings are held over the next sixty days. Citizens and local governments submit comments to the MMS on the adequacy of the

Principles of Public Participation

Keep the following principles in mind when participating in the lease sale process:

- Oppose OCS leasing in areas containing important renewable resources that OCS development would destroy or irreparably harm.

- Request the MMS to obtain and consider more and better information on the likely effects of oil development on the environment and socioeconomics before making the decision to lease.

- Request the MMS to disclose detailed information on the nature, extent, and location of offshore oil and gas resources and the likely location of onshore facilities prior to leasing for permit and planning purposes.

- Forbid OCS-related onshore development in fragile, undeveloped coastal areas.

- Forbid drilling in areas where oil spill containment and cleanup technology are not available or workable.

- Impose stringent environmental standards on existing operations in order to limit the possibility of blowouts, chronic spills, and operational discharges; require use of best available and safest technologies and practices in all operations, including transportation, that could lead to spills or that involve routine discharges, including air and water pollution.

document and the potential local impacts of the proposed lease sale.

Three to five months after the public hearings, the MMS issues a final environmental impact statement. A month later the "Proposed Notice of Sale" (PNOS) appears. This provides information on which blocks will be available for leasing, the stipulations for given blocks, the bidding system that will be used, and the terms of the lease.

The PNOS is sent to the governor, who is given sixty days to comment. At this stage, public hearings can be held by the state. The governor again consults with local governments in order to formulate a reply to the MMS's plan. Again, your input to your local representatives as well as the governor is crucial at this time.

The governor sends these comments to the Secretary of the Interior, who must consider them when making his final decision regarding the sale. After the response to the governor's comments, the "Final Notice of Sale" is issued. It includes sale times and places.

Though the Secretary of the Interior has the final say on where oil drilling will occur and under what conditions, public opinion greatly influences his decision. Citizens and local and state governments need to participate fully throughout the lease sale process in order to help shape the final outcome.

The timetable for lease sale steps changes frequently. It is vital that you receive the most up-to-date scheduling information. One way to do this is to be placed on the MMS mailing list and request advance notice about leasing schedules. The MMS occasionally publishes material that summarizes OCS activities. See Appendix D for the agency address.

Citizen action groups, environmental organizations, and local and state agencies can also provide you with timely information. They can help you understand just what the specific socioeconomic and environmental impacts of oil drilling will be on your local area. Staff members can provide you with information from experts in water quality, marine biology, engineering, oceanography, land use planning, and law. This kind of information is helpful when preparing your letters of comments for public hearings. In addition to providing written information, many citizen groups and local and state agencies sponsor workshops, meetings, and hearings on important aspects of the MMS leasing process. Look for notices announcing the time and place of meetings in organization flyers, newsletters, or public service announcements presented by local media. A list of citizen groups and their addresses and phone numbers can be found in Appendix D.

Scheduled hearings are not the only opportunities for making your opinions known about the government's plan to lease America's coast to the oil companies. Tell your local, state, and federal elected officials what you think. Write a letter to the editor of your local newspaper expressing your views, or, better yet, write an editorial for publication in the opinion section. Sample correspondence can be found in Appendix C.

2 DANGEROUS CURRENTS

How Offshore Drilling Affects Ecology and the Quality of Life

The environmental impacts of oil and gas production on the outer continental shelf (OCS) have been debated for many years. The issues arise from the complexity of coastal and offshore marine processes and ecosystems, human socioeconomic systems, and interactions with OCS oil and gas development activities. Mounting scientific evidence reveals that each step of offshore energy development—from exploration to drilling, from transport to refining—exposes land, air, and water to a host of pollutants. Hazardous wastes and air toxics are just a few of the harmful by-products that can affect marine life as well as the quality of life onshore.

The Department of the Interior's call to open the nation's coast to offshore drilling raises many questions: What are the effects of toxic and other waste generated by drilling? What are the risks of oil spills fouling the nation's coast? What will the impact be on marine wildlife and the commercial fishery? How will the tourist industry be affected? Will the coast become industrialized? Are there alternatives to offshore oil drilling? Each of these issues is addressed in the following pages.

Oil Spills

Offshore drilling causes oil spills. Between 1964 and 1985, twenty-one major spills involving one thousand barrels or more occurred as a result of drilling and production operations on the OCS. Those numbers are sure to increase if more sites are opened to drilling. The DOI estimated that twenty-two to forty-six major spills would occur as a result of the 1987-92 five-year program. New oil drilling off the coast of Southern California, for example, would increase the chance of a large oil spill in the region appreciably and make a major spill almost certain within the next thirty-one years, according to a DOI assessment. The study found one chance in seven of a "large" spill of one thousand barrels. The probability of one or more major spills occurring from all OCS activities off Southern California is 99+ percent.

Those risk estimates don't even take into consideration spills under one thousand barrels, even though such spills make up 97 percent of all spills. The DOI does not input data of spills of this size into its Oil Spill Risk Analysis (OSRA), a computer model used to estimate risk. This

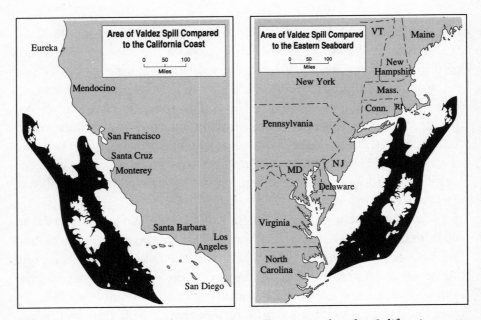

FIGURES 3 and 4 *Area of Exxon Valdez spill compared to the California coast and the Eastern Seaboard.*

Source: Central Coast Regional Studies Program

means that official risk estimates contained in environmental impact statements—key documents prepared before deciding whether or not to drill in specific areas—can underestimate the likelihood of an oil spill by a factor of as much as 260.

According to a 1989 report issued by the National Academy of Sciences, the DOI's OSRA is fatally flawed. The NAS found that the DOI lacks important scientific information about physical oceanography on which oil spill risk estimates are based. The NAS report concluded that "[m]odel studies need to be supplemented with observations. Trajectory predictions or estimations of trajectory statistics realistic for use in risk analysis or in accident management cannot be obtained without new fieldwork. . . ."

The report also faulted DOI for relying "too heavily upon the OSRA model for prediction of impacts. This has resulted in an emphasis on the probability of an oil spill instead of on the effects of a spill."

Spill Sources

A variety of sources during offshore development and production can trigger an oil spill, including tanker accidents, well blowouts, pipeline leaks, and routine operations.

Tankers. Tanker mishaps are the leading cause of spills. Take the six-month period between December 1988 and June 1989, for example. Six major oil spills off the U.S. coast were caused by ships. On December 22 a collision between two vessels caused 230,000 gallons of oil to spill off Washington's Olympic Peninsula. On March 3 the oil tanker *Exxon Houston* struck a coral reef near Honolulu and spilled 117,000 gallons of fuel. Three weeks later its sister ship, the *Exxon Valdez*, ran aground in Prince William Sound, flooding the pristine waters with nearly 11 million gallons of Alaskan crude. On June 23, about one million gallons of fuel began washing ashore in Newport, Rhode Island, from a grounded Greek tanker. That same day, 250,000 gallons of heavy crude oil were spilled in the Houston Ship Channel near Galveston, Texas, when a tug-driven barge collided with a cargo vessel. And the next day, an Uruguayan oil tanker spilled 800,000 gallons of fuel into the Delaware River.

According to the U.S. Coast Guard, there were 981 accidents involving tankers registered in the United States from 1981 through 1988, including 175 collisions. During that same time 413 foreign-registered tankers were involved in accidents in U.S. waters.

Millions of gallons of oil are dumped into U.S. waters each year as a result. In 1988, there were five thousand to six thousand spills involving oil and other toxic substances along our coasts and in other navigable waters, says the Coast Guard. Of those spills, twelve were classified as major because they involved 100,000 gallons or more. An additional ten spilled 10,000 to 100,000 gallons, and the rest involved less than 10,000 gallons. Data from the Coast Guard's Pollution Incident Reporting System reveal that 91 million gallons of oil and 36 million gallons of other toxic substances were spilled into U.S. waters from 1980 through 1986. Of the spilled oil, two-thirds came from oil tankers and barges, usually because of ruptures in accidents. The rest came from offshore drilling platforms, refineries, and other sources such as runoff and tank ballast washings.

Human error, according to the Coast Guard, is responsible for most of the accidents. Though spills do result from negligence by intoxicated crew members, most accidents are made by well-trained seamen and have nothing to do with drugs or alcohol or incompetence.

Tankers are vulnerable to all kinds of accidents caused by human error. On February 7, 1990, for example, the *American Trader* spilled about 400,000 gallons of Alaskan crude off the Southern California coast when it apparently struck its own anchor. The tanker punctured its hull while trying to hook up with a mooring buoy and unload its cargo via an underwater pipeline that feeds refineries and tank farms along the coast.

Drilling platforms. Offshore rigs contribute significantly to the total amount of oil spilled in U.S. waters. During drilling there is a risk of a blowout, an uncontrolled discharge of oil from the drill hole. A blowout can occur when, because of equipment failure, human error, or unpredicted geological conditions, the pressure in the underground oil reservoir cannot be contained.

The most famous U.S. blowout took place in California's Santa Barbara Channel in 1969. It happened when Union Oil was drilling nearly one mile below the ocean's floor. The protective casing used to line the 5,000-foot deep well was only 240 feet long—too short to control the pressure of surging oil. The drill's bit went through a fracture in the rock and the pressurized oil shot out through the fissures. The pressure was so great that it blasted a hole in the seabed 200 yards away from the well. For twelve days oil gushed unchecked into the ocean. Some 50,000 to

Photo from Central Coast Regional Studies Program

Offshore drilling platforms are enormous steel structures that can tower as high as the Empire State Building.

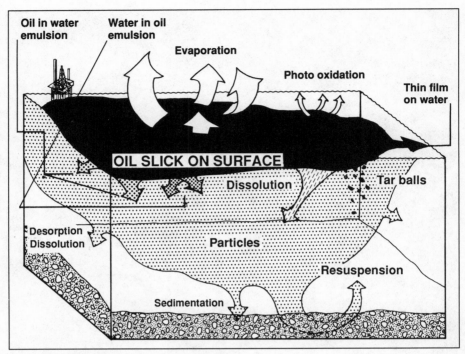

FIGURE 5 *The anatomy of an oil spill.*
Source: Washington Sea Grant Program

70,000 barrels of oil spread over 660 square miles, fouling 150 miles of coastline and leaving thousands of dead birds, mammals, and fish in its wake.

Oil can also leak from holding tanks on board the drilling platforms. Earthquakes, vessel collisions, structural failures, human and operational errors, and mechanical defects can rupture storage tanks.

Oil is also discharged into the sea from the produced water—water in the formation that is produced along with oil. Produced water often contains large amounts of dissolved or emulsified oil and grease, as much as thousands of barrels a year.

Pipelines. The pipelines used to transfer the oil from the platform to either offshore or onshore processing plants are also vulnerable to leaks and ruptures. Corrosion, being struck by a ship's anchor, and mechanical defects are the leading causes for the majority of all pipeline failures. Pipeline leaks can also be triggered by earthquakes, internal corrosion, and human error.

Spill Cleanup

A variety of techniques are used in efforts to contain, recover, and clean up oil once it is spilled. Specially equipped boats are used to skim the oil from the surface. Floating booms are placed around the edges of the slick to corral it. In some cases chemical dispersants are sprayed over the slick to try to break the oil down to speed up natural degradation and weathering. Sometimes the oil is even ignited. The latter two techniques are controversial, however. Many experts say they can cause more harm than good. Some chemical dispersants, for instance, are toxic to wildlife. When oil washes ashore, cleanup becomes a more labor-intensive job: Cleaners must sponge up the oil with absorbents such as hay, and wash and scrub beaches by hand. A new cleanup technique that is being tried involves stimulating the growth of naturally occurring oil eating bacteria. Called bioremediation, this technique has shown promise in bench-scale testing situations and in limited field experiments.

According to the DOI estimates, only 5 to 15 percent of oil from a spill can be recovered or cleaned up, on the average. Cleanup failure is due to many factors, including inclement weather, limited technology, technical problems, and human mismanagement. The *Exxon Valdez* spill proved how difficult it is to clean up oil once it is spilled. The slick from the 257,000-barrel, or 10.8-million-gallon, spill contaminated 1,244 miles of shoreline. Despite a six-month-long cleanup effort waged by 11,000 people, 1,000 vessels, and more than 70 aircraft at a cost of more than $1.9 billion, little of the spilled oil was removed. Only 32,500 barrels of oil were recovered and possibly 77,100 barrels evaporated. That means more than 147,000 barrels, or 6.17 million gallons, remain in the environment.

Contingency plans developed by industry and the government to deal with large oil spills have proved woefully inadequate. When the *Exxon Valdez* floundered on Bligh Reef, for example, eight oil spill contingency plans were in effect that had relevance to the spill response effort. These included several federal plans, the state of Alaska's plan, and a plan coordinated by Alyeska, the coalition of oil companies that jointly operate the Trans-Alaska Pipeline and Valdez oil terminal. However, a team of investigators from the Center for Marine Conservation found serious flaws in many aspects of these plans. For instance, the plans lacked important details in describing where and how to deploy booms

1969 Santa Barbara photo by Bud Bottoms

for excluding oil from sensitive areas. Nor did the plans contain current information on the location of necessary equipment and supplies, contractors, and vendors. The center's report concluded that federal agency contingency plans frequently give vague or conflicting guidance on what degree of response is appropriate, particularly in the case of spills in which the response has not been federalized.

Beach cleanup technologies have changed little since the 1969 Santa Barbara oil spill.

Spills much smaller than the *Exxon Valdez* spill are also resistant to cleanup efforts. For example, when the tanker *Puerto Rican* exploded outside San Francisco's Golden Gate Bridge in 1984, spilling an estimated 400,000 gallons of oil, less than 5 percent of the spill was contained. Much of the cleanup failure was blamed on the area's weather conditions, typified by high seas and fast currents. The six-foot-high seas interfered with skimming operations, and currents from 1 to 1.5 knots prevented portable booms from halting the spread of oil. The slick drifted northward to the Gulf of Farallones National Marine Sanctuary, the largest seabird rookery in the continental United States, killing thousands of seabirds, including such sensitive species as the common murre and Cassin's auklet. The California Coastal Commission, a state agency that has permitting authority over activities in the state's coastal zone, has concluded that "a large open ocean oil spill cannot be cleaned up offshore using technology now available."

Most frontier areas that the DOI has targeted for drilling are not quickly accessible by cleanup crews. This compounds the problem of controlling a spill should one occur.

Long-term Impacts

While some spilled oil degrades naturally—the amount depends on several factors, including the type of oil, prevailing weather conditions, water temperature, salinity, current, and location—the remainder can linger in the environment as a source of chronic pollution for years, even decades. Long-term exposure to oil causes many biological problems, including depressed birth rates and genetic mutations in certain populations of marine species.

Scientists studying the aftereffects of the *Amoco Cadiz* wreck reported in *Science* magazine that the 67.2-million-gallon spill was still contaminating the Brittany coast a decade after the American supertanker went aground in March 1978. As late as 1984, sediments in estuaries contained as much as 100 parts per million of polycyclic hydrocarbons, a level considered toxic to oysters and other invertebrates.

The results of this long-term contamination were most noticeable in several marine species. Oyster flesh contained 200 parts per million of the contaminant. This resulted in the intentional destruction of five thousand tons of oysters in 1978—oysters that would have been marketed for human consumption. According to *New Scientist*, the chronic pollution also caused a significant proportion of the population of plaice, a commercial species of flatfish, to develop defective ovaries. Some ovaries were immature when they should have been ripe; some had empty egg follicles; and some had masses of connective tissue and blood vessels rather than reproductive cells. Reproductive failure limited the size of the plaice population.

Another study chronicling the long-term persistence of oil in marine sediments involves a spill that occurred off the coast of Massachusetts. The barge *Florida* ran aground on a rocky shoal off West Falmouth on September 16, 1969, spilling 170,000 gallons of fuel. The slick spread over more than one thousand acres, including four miles of coastline. Marine scientists from Woods Hole Oceanographic Institute found that, as years passed, the oil did not disappear, but spread through sediments to other areas and affected wetland populations. Traces of the fuel could still be found in wetland sediments twenty years after the spill. *Audubon* magazine reported that one of the most disturbing outward signs of the chronic pollution was exhibited by fiddler crabs. Although those animals were not killed in great numbers at first, many aberrations appeared in

Oil spills are deadly to seabirds. When coated, they lose their buoyancy and drown.

the survivors, including increased molting, out-of-season breeding color display, and impaired locomotion and escape response. Probably the most destructive aberration was the crabs' failure to dig burrows deep enough to protect themselves from freezing in winter. The oil caused the reduction of fiddler crab populations for at least seven years.

Oil spill recovery rates slow in cold water. Oil frozen into the sea ice and released during thaws can prolong the effects of a spill. Researchers writing in *Applied and Environmental Microbiology* estimate that crude oil spilled in cold waters like those found in Alaska can cause measurable effects on microbial function for up to six years after the initial impact. Their data suggest that oil pollution reduces the production of bacterial biomass, or biosynthesis, in marine sediments. The impact to benthic, or bottom-dwelling, organisms, which consume bacteria as part of their diet, disrupts the very base of the marine food chain.

Photo by Marion Stirrup

Water Quality

Offshore drilling and production operations generate huge quantities of waste. According to the National Academy of Sciences, drilling a single well produces between 1,500 to 2,000 tons of waste materials. These wastes are not the result of accidents but are the by-products of routine operations. Current regulations allow companies operating around the nation to discharge the equivalent of up to twenty-five separate oil spills of one thousand barrels each in wastewater and up to 15 million pounds of toxic metals in drilling waste. Drilling mud used during drilling operations to lubricate and cool the drill bit, control underground pressure, and remove drill cuttings—pieces of ground-up rock—contain toxic materials.

The DOI estimates that additional drilling activities in the Southern California planning area, for instance, will "result in the discharge of approximately 2.7 million gallons of drilling muds and cuttings." Again, these are the routine by-products of operations.

Oil and gas production also produces wastewater that can be contaminated by oil, grease, cadmium, benzene, lead, and other toxic organics and metals. These materials can poison aquatic organisms and waterfowl. The wastewater is usually dumped right into the ocean. Oil industry data indicate that over 1.5 million barrels of wastewater were discharged into the Gulf of Mexico each day in 1986.

Wastewater often contains carcinogenic aromatic hydrocarbon compounds, including benzene and naphthalene. An Environmental Protection Agency study of wastewater discharges in the Gulf of Mexico found naphthalene in concentrations of 1.5 parts per million. That is one hundred times the level found by the U.S. Fish and Wildlife Service to be toxic to fish eggs and benthic organisms.

Toxic materials added to drilling fluids include bactericides, soluble salts, mineral oil, and ethylene glycol. Mixing and disposing the materials together can produce a synergistic effect that can increase their toxicity. This practice poses a hazard to both fish and birds.

Research conducted by the EPA shows that drilling wastes harm a variety of marine organisms in many ways. Scientists at the University of California at Santa Barbara discovered that even small concentrations of drilling wastes can interfere with the food-finding ability of such commercially important species of shellfish as spiny lobsters.

Drilling wastes disposed on the seafloor suffocate benthic organisms in a pancake of death. They also strip the surrounding water of oxygen. Oxygen is essential not only to keep marine organisms alive but also to sustain species reproduction and vigor. The EPA estimates that the total annual biochemical oxygen demand (BOD) in drilling wastes may be more than six times higher than the total BOD of all ocean-dumped municipal sewage sludge. Reduced dissolved oxygen concentrations interfere with fish populations through delayed hatching of eggs, reduced size and vigor of embryos, deformities in young, and other severe effects. Severely depressed oxygen levels kill life forms and eliminate their habitat.

Recent concerns have been raised about radioactivity in produced water. Radioactive material can be leached into produced water from uranium and thorium in deep geological formations and brought to the surface in oil and gas operations. Studies by the Louisiana Department of Environmental Quality indicate that produced water often contains levels of radioactivity above what can be legally discharged from a nuclear power plant. Radioactivity is trapped in scale caked inside used pipes, causing the pipes to become radioactive. High levels of radioactivity also have been found in oil field waste pits used for produced water discharge in Louisiana.

Air Quality

Offshore platforms and onshore support facilities belch large amounts of pollutants into the air, including oxides of nitrogen (NO_x) and reactive hydrocarbons, which react chemically to create ozone, the principal component of photochemical smog. Smog poses serious threats to public health. Symptoms include irritation of the respiratory system, coughing, wheezing, headaches, as well as aggravation of asthma, bronchitis, and emphysema. Additional health-risking pollutants include carbon monoxide (CO) and oxides of sulfur—a precursor of acid rain.

Sources of air pollution include the diesel generators and engines used to power supply boats, well-drilling equipment, and other machinery. Emissions from these internal combustion machines pollute the air just as cars and trucks do. At a single site during well testing, for example, uncontrolled emissions of NO_x from the diesel equipment can be over three thousand pounds per day.

Construction activities also produce polluting vapors. Again, NO_x emissions are the greatest concern. If offshore development is allowed to take place along the Central California coast, for example, NO_x emissions during construction would average up to 2,500 pounds per day over a period of six months, with a maximum daily amount approaching four tons per day. That would equal the NO_x emissions currently being produced by all the cars and trucks registered in nearby Sonoma County.

Offshore oil storage and treatment facilities (OS&Ts), the large floating factory ships used to process oil, are big air polluters, too. Storage tanks and valves leak fugitive hydrocarbon emissions. The tankers they service produce NO_x, CO, and sulfur dioxide (SO_2).

Onshore, air pollution comes from oil treatment plants. Every day they generate NO_x, SO_2, and CO.

In most coastal areas, state-regulated onshore air pollution control requirements are more stringent than federal laws governing platforms and OS&Ts operating beyond the three-mile limit. Yet the emissions produced by these offshore facilities blow to shore and can prevent some coastal communities from meeting state clean air standards. This can affect a state's ability to plan for new industry and business activity unrelated to offshore development.

The Greenhouse Effect

Offshore oil development adds to global warming, commonly called the greenhouse effect. According to government studies, the daily emissions from one exploratory drilling rig can equal seven thousand cars driving fifty miles. Automobile-type emissions account for about 25 percent of the amount of carbon dioxide emitted into the air in the United States. CO_2 is a principal "greenhouse" gas.

Current emissions of these gases far exceed the ability of forests and oceans to absorb them. Every year fossil-fuel combustion, such as in cars and trucks, and the oil and diesel fuel used to power offshore platform generators, drill ships, and onshore production facilities, generate five billion tons of carbon emissions. Natural mechanisms remove only about half the total. Atmospheric carbon concentrations have increased from their historical level of about 270 parts per million to about 345 parts per million.

The National Academy of Sciences estimates that the temperature of the earth's atmosphere will increase between 2.7 and 8.1 degrees Fahrenheit as a result of such human-made gases in the next fifty to one hundred years. Even at the low end of this range, the increase would bring global average temperatures to a level not seen in six thousand years. At the high end, we would have to adjust, within less than a century, to average temperatures present during the age of the dinosaurs.

Effects will vary from region to region. San Francisco Bay will grow saltier, soybean crops around the Great Lakes will become more robust, and coastal cities like Miami will need more storm sewers, if not dikes, says a report by the EPA. One government model predicts the number of days above 95 degrees Fahrenheit in the Corn Belt will triple if the average temperature rises only three degrees globally. Reduced crop yields would result. *The Wall Street Journal* reports that in California's Central Valley, which accounts for 10 percent of U.S. agriculture, irrigation will have to be increased as spring runoff from the Sierra Mountains decreases.

Destruction of most of the country's forests and flooding of 80 percent of our coastal wetlands are also likely to occur. A two-foot rise in sea level caused by global warming would force salt water into coastal drinking water systems and cause massive, sudden, and violent changes in the economy and usability of shorelines worldwide.

Construction costs to compensate for these changes would be high. Costs to protect developed shorelines could reach $111 billion through the year 2100 if the sea level rises one meter, according to the EPA report. The EPA estimates sea-level increases by that year at half a meter to two meters, and says that despite efforts to protect shoreline, an area the size of New Jersey could be lost. More severe summer heat will increase demand for electricity, which could require spending $325 billion to build power plants.

Global warming would affect animal and plant life, as well as human life. Human mortality rates would be altered by the changing climate's effect on contagious diseases that are influenced by the weather, like influenza. Respiratory diseases might become more severe as ozone air pollution increases in warmer temperatures.

Wildlife

Marine life is seriously jeopardized by offshore energy development activities. Oil spills pose the most readily apparent risk. As *Exxon Valdez* demonstrated, sea otters are extremely vulnerable to spilled oil. The spill

Photo by John Hyde, Alaska Department of Fish and Game

Sea otters are especially vulnerable to oil spills. They die of hypothermia when between 20 to 30 percent of their bodies are coated with oil, and they die from ingesting the oil while trying to clean their coats.

killed an estimated one thousand otters. The otters depend on their insulating fur for survival in the chilling seas and will almost certainly die of hypothermia when between 20 to 30 percent of their bodies are coated with oil. Rehabilitating oiled otters is difficult. Nearly one-third of the 354 otters captured in Prince William Sound after the spill died despite heroic rehabilitation efforts. Necropsies and pathology studies revealed that the animals that died in the first weeks of rehabilitation had severely damaged internal organs and deficient immune systems. Part of the cause was thought to be the stress of capture and handling, but the toxic effects of inhaled, ingested, and absorbed fumes and oil appeared to have killed most of the animals.

Oil affects most species of seabirds the same way as otters. Once coated, a bird can lose its buoyancy and drown, or it can become poisoned from ingesting the oil while trying to preen its feathers. The impact of a spill in key breeding areas can be catastrophic. The total known bird mortality in Prince William Sound from the *Exxon Valdez* spill was roughly 33,000. And that's just the carcasses that could be counted. No doubt thousands more were not recovered. According to the Center for Marine Conservation at Katmai National Park, five hundred miles from Bligh Reef, dead birds were washing up onshore in concentrations of two thousand to three thousand per mile. The DOI documents reveal that ingestion of oil also significantly reduces reproduction in some birds, and that contamination of eggs by oil-fouled feathers of parent birds reduces egg-hatching success.

Invertebrates are vulnerable to oiling, too. Filter feeders like clams, oysters, and crabs ingest the poisonous substance and die. The effect of oiling is especially hard felt in tropical ecosystems like the coral reefs off Florida. Coral polyps, the tiny animals that make reefs, display a wide range of responses to oil, including massive outright destruction, decreases in reproduction and colonization capacity, and changes in feeding and behavior. Experiments reveal that certain types of corals exposed to fuel show reduced and varied growth between heads. This is significant, because a coral's success at tolerating grazing and predation as well as its ability to compete for space is dependent largely upon its growth.

Another tropical genus extremely vulnerable to spilled oil is the mangrove. Portions of the nation's southeastern coastline are forested with these tropical trees. When contaminated by oil, the openings in the trees' aerial root systems become clogged, thus limiting their ability to take in nutrients. Mangrove trees generally require a minimum of twenty years to recover after being damaged this way.

Fish eggs, fry, and smolts are easily poisoned by very low oil concentrations. The most poisonous components found in oil—the aromatic hydrocarbons—are toxic to fish eggs at the parts per billion level, U.S. Fish and Wildlife Service documents reveal. Adult fish are also vulnerable to oil spills. Fish absorb oil in their fatty tissues. English sole develop cancerous tumors when exposed to oil. Eating oil-contaminated fish is a health hazard.

Wildlife species formally designated as endangered or threatened risk extinction from offshore drilling. They are vulnerable not only to oil spills but also to day-to-day operations. Platforms require an average of two helicopter trips per day during installation, development drilling, and production. Construction of an offshore pipeline requires additional daily chopper trips.

Helicopters, seismic exploration activities, boat traffic, and drilling operations can disturb birds, whales, and other animals, causing them to leave and stay away. For example, helicopter and other air traffic to and from OCS operations in the St. George Basin in Alaska's Bering Sea resulted in severe disturbance of waterfowl in the Izembek Lagoon National Wildlife Refuge. The same effect can be expected if the DOI allows drilling platforms to be built off California's North Coast. The noise could drive away existing colonies of small murres, a sensitive seabird species.

Noise caused by underwater blasting and drilling can damage the extremely sensitive hearing of whales and seals. Research in the Beaufort Sea reveals that endangered bowhead whales avoid drilling and seismic activities. The National Marine Fisheries Service has concluded that operations in certain areas of the Beaufort could "block or seriously disrupt" the whales' spring migration, thus jeopardizing their existence. Experiments show that the hair cells of the auditory organs of some fish are destroyed by high noise levels. Underwater noise forces fish to flee, damages eggs, and reduces the growth of fry. Prolonged effects to commercial species of fish may ultimately reduce the catches of commercial fishermen.

According to the National Academy of Sciences, the DOI has based its decision to lease specific areas on inadequate scientific information concerning the effects of oil and gas production on wildlife. In a 1989 report to the White House, the NAS found that the DOI lacks general biological process studies; does not pay enough attention to inshore, onshore, and estuarine areas; has too narrow a focus on oil spills and not enough on the other potential impacts associated with development and production; overestimates potential recovery rates of ecosystems after damage in its environmental impact statements; and has largely ignored sublethal and chronic effects of oil and gas activities.

Onshore Industrialization

Offshore oil development isn't restricted to offshore. In fact, drilling results in marine industrialization of onshore areas. Offshore oil requires construction of supply bases, roads, helicopter landing pads, pipelines, processing plants, and employee housing onshore. These activities affect scenic, cultural, and natural resources and result in increased demand for existing public services.

Construction of a supply base, for example, degrades the environment in several ways. The typical supply base requires up to thirty-five acres of coastal land. Construction and operation displace aquatic and terrestrial species. Increased traffic from trucks, helicopters, and ships generates noise pollution. Gasoline and diesel-powered equipment contributes to onshore air pollution levels. Solid and hazardous waste disposal affects ground and surface water.

Pipelines also displace aquatic and terrestrial species. Onshore, a pipeline requires a corridor up to one hundred feet wide for right of way during construction and a thirty- to fifty-foot-wide corridor during operation. For each linear mile of pipeline, about six acres of vegetation are destroyed.

The impacts associated with pipelines include degradation of surface water, archaeological resources, slope stability, coastal lagoons, and wetlands. Excavation and placement of a pipeline leave permanent visible scars across coastal lands in some places and cause erosion where the pipeline exits the sea to cross beach areas and move inland through coastal bluffs.

Pipelines placed on the seafloor disturb seabed habitat and kelp beds and can interfere with commercial fishing. For each pipeline, approximately a fifteen-hundred-foot right of way is disturbed. Where pipelines

Photo by Tyler Johnson

Dramatic alteration of onshore environments accompanies offshore drilling.

Onshore pipeline construction has major environmental impacts.

Photo by John Storrer, County of Santa Barbara

cross kelp beds, all kelp plants within a fifteen-hundred-foot corridor could be damaged. Kelp plants could take more than five years to reestablish. The loss of habitat reduces dependent fish and invertebrate populations.

Separation and treatment facilities located onshore can require up to 140 acres of flat land. Construction usually involves grading, which destroys existing vegetation. The highly visible buildings degrade visual resources. They also require significant amounts of energy for production purposes. An increase in air pollutants results.

The plants use massive amounts of fresh water for processing as well. Projected water use for a 200,000-barrel-a-day facility ranges from 112 to 425 acre feet per year. In comparison, the average single family residence uses about half an acre foot of water per year. The plants also discharge wastewater. Often the wastewater is flushed directly into the ocean, where it can lower biological productivity and accumulates in bottom sediments. Onshore, uncontrolled wastewater can leach into groundwater, a common source of drinking water.

Ocean water quality is affected by marine terminals and storage tanks used to load and offload oil to and from tankers. Marine terminals require large amounts of onshore and offshore space to accommodate storage tanks, subsea oil and gas pipelines from the tanks to a floating offshore loading station, power transmission systems for moving the product to the tanker and supplying other energy needs for the terminal and tanker, and buoys and anchoring systems. The terminals affect coastal visual resources, contribute to air and water pollution, and compete with recreational boaters and commercial fishermen for docking space.

Socioeconomics

Offshore oil and gas exploration, development, and production affect the socioeconomics of a region in a number of ways. Yet, according to a report issued by the National Academy of Sciences, the DOI routinely performs inadequate social and economic analyses prior to making the decision to lease an area to oil companies.

In standard practice, social and economic analyses of natural resource development focus on the direct and secondary impacts associated with development and production, as well as the related infrastructure and public financing requirements. These analyses deal primarily with impacts that are quantifiable, often in economic terms. However, the NAS says such analyses "were not systematically carried out by the DOI." The report goes on to explain:

- The DOI's data often were not current, not useful at the local level, and not analyzed in a way that helps decision making. In addition, few long-term studies have been carried out. Despite the abundant experience with OCS development and production, there has been little follow-up research to validate socioeconomic assumptions and conclusions.
- Significant types of social and economic impacts have been ignored. Different kinds of social and economic impacts other than those that the DOI has addressed can occur from OCS activities. Some begin even before a lease sale is held. There is no program to systematically study and evaluate this class of impacts, and they have not even been considered in the environmental impact statements.

The mere announcement of a lease sale can raise fear and uncertainty, stimulate organized political resistance, encourage land speculation, lead to lawsuits, and result in widespread anger and alienation among citizens who feel that their rights are being violated and their ways of life threatened.

Commercial Fishing

Offshore energy development conflicts with commercial fishing. Oil companies locate oil and gas deposits offshore by using seismic survey boats that tow long strings of sonic equipment behind them. The Pacific Coast Federation of Fishermen's Association complains that "streamers" cut off buoys attached to such commercial fishing gear as traps and set nets and tangle with troll lines.

The survey vessels cause fish to disperse as well, and can result in catch losses. This phenomenon has been verified by several studies, including one conducted by the Battelle/Marine Research Laboratory for the Minerals Management Service. The Battelle test showed total catch declined by 52.4 percent after seismic surveying. The sonic pulses emitted by survey ships harm fish and shellfish, particularly during the egg and larval stages.

Installation of offshore drilling platforms displaces traditional fishing grounds when they are located in such areas. The rigs require a tremendous amount of space. A single exploratory drill ship can usurp a one- to six-mile fishing area with its anchor lines, and a platform can take up between five to twenty square miles with its anchor cables, underwater pipelines, and buffer zones. The deeper the water, the wider the area the rig requires. In the Santa Barbara Channel of California, for instance, Pacific Coast Federation fishermen estimate that over 40 percent of the trawl grounds have been lost to drilling platforms.

Displacement makes fishermen spend more time and money looking for new fishing areas. The reduction of fishing grounds increases pressure on remaining areas. The ensuing competition leads to declines in average vessel operating efficiency and productivity.

Reduced catches affect onshore fish processing plants. The economic well-being of these facilities is tied directly to the success of the fishing fleet. The impact from a drop in catch reverberates through the entire economy.

The claim that oil rigs and platforms act as artificial reefs and attract fish has little benefit to the commercial fishing industry. Fishing vessels are forbidden to enter "safety zones" surrounding the rigs. Even if they could, the drilling rigs' cables and anchors would foul their nets.

Near shore, commercial fishing faces increased competition for dock space and onshore support facilities from OCS construction barges, supply vessels, crew boats, tankers, and processing ships. The increased demand for berthing space drives up prices and raises commercial fishing operating expenses.

Oil spills can severely affect commercial fishing. The Center for Marine Conservation discovered that the *Exxon Valdez* spill affected a $110-million fishery and the additional $260 million in economic activities associated with it. The direct effects of the spill included several total or partial fishery closures to keep nets and fish species from becoming oiled. Following the spill, all salmon net fisheries in Prince William Sound were closed pending further evaluation of the extent of oil pollution. Some salmon areas in nearby Cook Inlet and almost all of the salmon fisheries at Kodiak Island were also closed. Herring fisheries in Prince William Sound, Gulf of Alaska, and Cook Inlet were also affected.

Closings are just part of the fallout from oil spills. Other impacts include direct toxic effects to eggs, fry, and smolt, which can lead to reduced catches in subsequent years. There is also a problem of market confidence in fish caught in spill areas. Fish contaminated by an oil spill in one area could drive down prices for an entire region.

Tourism

Offshore oil development poses a serious threat to coastal areas dependent upon tourism for economic survival. Oil spills are especially threatening to areas where natural and cultural resources, scenic beauty, and outdoor recreation attract visitors who support inns, restaurants, retail shops, recreational outlets, and other local services.

Consider the *Exxon Valdez* spill, for example. The director of the Valdez Convention and Visitors Bureau told an investigating team from the Center for Marine Conservation that tourist-related businesses in Valdez were "hurt and hurt bad." The total number of tourists visiting Valdez after the spill dropped between 30 and 50 percent. A cruise line canceled its sixteen scheduled stops in Valdez for 1990 because of problems obtaining berthing space during 1989. The Anchorage branch of the American Automobile Association told motorists not to visit Valdez because of problems caused by the spill and cleanup efforts. Hotel space and airline seats were dominated by spill workers, leaving tour operators unable to assure travelers of transportation and accommodations. True,

Photo by Chris Calwell

Recreation and tourism support healthy coastal economies.

hotels and airlines did not suffer immediate financial impacts from the spill, but once spill workers left, there was potential for long-term damage due to an absence of tourism.

Construction and operation of offshore platforms and onshore support facilities also affect tourism. Offshore platforms and onshore refineries diminish visual resources. The increased traffic from helicopters, trucks, and boats leads to higher noise levels. Processing plants smell. Onshore industrialization detracts from "scenic beauty and peace and quiet," key commodities depended upon by the tourist trade.

Intensive drilling along the mid-Atlantic coast, for instance, would compromise the region's principal attraction, a 1,000-mile shoreline made up of sandy beaches and barrier islands that draws millions of tourists annually. Tourism or travel for the purpose of recreation is a mainstay of the economy of virtually all the counties along this largely rural coastline. A 1,200-mile-long oil slick like the one caused by the *Exxon Valdez* would affect every community along the entire coastline here.

Florida's tourist-based economy is also jeopardized by drilling plans. The southwest Florida shelf lies adjacent to Everglades National Park, the Florida Keys, two national marine sanctuaries, two national wildlife sanctuaries, a national natural landmark, two national wilderness areas, and an aquatic preserve. These natural resources draw over one million out-of-state tourists each year. They spend millions of dollars on hotels, food, rental of diving equipment, and other services. Yet this area has the highest chance of land contact should a spill occur in the eastern Gulf of Mexico, according to government documents.

A drop in tourism affects more than just inns, restaurants, and retail stores. According to the California Department of Commerce, total tourist spending along the Central California coast generates approximately $7.8 billion in revenues, 140,000 jobs, and approximately $400 million in state and local taxes each year. Coastal communities depend on tourism for significant portions of their public revenues. The city of San Francisco obtains an estimated $13.8 million from coastal hotel taxes each year. In Carmel-by-the-Sea, more than 50 percent of the city's revenues are considered tourist-based.

Jobs

The claim that offshore oil development creates job opportunities for local workers is largely unfounded. Experience demonstrates that only minimal employment opportunities for the local labor pool are produced. Most of the jobs go to workers in other states who are employed by drilling equipment manufacturing firms or, increasingly, to workers in other countries.

For example, most contracts for the construction of the large skeletal frameworks that support the deck sections of platforms have been awarded to foreign contractors in recent years because of their ability to produce goods at a lower cost. According to a 1985 U.S. International Trade Commission report, only one of ten platforms to be used off the West Coast that was put out to bid by the industry since 1979 was awarded to a domestic fabricator. Steel industry officials report that almost 20 percent of the active rigs in the Gulf of Mexico in 1985 were produced abroad.

Operation of drilling platforms doesn't provide many local job opportunities, either. The rigs are highly automated and require specialized skills to run them. While each production platform requires approximately two hundred workers during the well-drilling phase, only a few operation and maintenance workers are needed once production begins. Jobs are typically filled by experienced oil-field hands brought in from oil-producing regions such as Oklahoma, Louisiana, and Texas. The high unemployment rate among oil workers in those states guarantees that the practice will continue for some years to come.

The capital benefits of drilling operations do not stay in a region, either; they are exported. Studies show that most workers brought in to run platforms maintain homes outside the region and return to them during their off-work time.

Nor do tax revenues generated by oil industry activity offset the expense borne by local taxpayers for the public services necessary to support the temporary swelling of the work force caused by construction activities.

True, oil spills often create employment opportunities—the workers are needed for cleanup—but the jobs are temporary. What's more, the jobs are usually filled at the expense of other businesses. The Center for Marine Conservation's investigation of the *Exxon Valdez* spill disclosed that many existing businesses had trouble retaining workers or finding new ones. They could not compete with the high wages that Exxon was paying. Many business leaders feared their businesses might fail as a result.

The spill created additional city expenses, too, the Center's report concluded. In just one month, the city had spill-related expenses of over $130,000. Another cost to the city had to do with wastes. According to news reports in the *Valdez Vanguard*, the need to incinerate an unexpectedly large quantity of waste caused seventy-five thousand dollars' worth of damage to the town's incinerator. The city's landfill also became overburdened by the cleanup. About five times the normal amount of waste was sent to the landfill. The waste generated by the increased population of Valdez, coupled with the waste from the spill cleanup crews' berthing ships, reduced the landfill's life by half. The cost of a new landfill? One million dollars.

Other Valdez city services also bore the brunt of the increased work force, including police services and the justice system. Arrests jumped by 500 percent, and in the first six weeks immediately following the spill, Valdez owed its police force 1,245 hours of overtime compared with 130 hours for all of 1988. The Valdez Superior Court had to schedule twice as many court days as normal, the *Valdez Vanguard* reported. Jail capacity was stretched to the limit.

3 HOLES IN THE SEA

How Offshore Oil and Gas Are Developed

Offshore oil and gas are developed in a five-phase cycle: leasing, exploration, development, production, and shutdown. The offshore oil industry is dominated by large, multinational companies that operate in a global market through complex organizational structures comprising national subsidiaries and affiliates. Smaller independent companies contract with these large firms to perform such technical and support operations as surveying, drilling, construction, and maintenance. It is not unusual for large multinationals, contractors, subcontractors, and even sub-subcontractors to work simultaneously on a single platform, an arrangement that can make it difficult to determine environmental liability.

Because oil companies play such a decisive role in the lease sale process, it is important for citizens to understand just how the industry works and how oil and gas are developed offshore.

Exploration

Oil and gas were formed millions of years ago when large volumes of dead organisms became trapped between successive layers of earth. As sedimentary rock continued to pile on top, the organic matter was cooked by a combination of heat and pressure into petroleum. Gradually the petroleum migrated into porous and permeable rocks, capped by impermeable layers, that act as reservoirs far below the earth's surface.

Surveying

Geologists prospect for black gold on board large survey ships that have been equipped with a sophisticated array of electronic gear. The ships plow the seas shooting sound blasts from air guns, or "sparkers," at the sea bottom. The acoustic waves penetrate deep into the earth's surface and are recorded as they bounce off the submarine geological layers by receivers attached to two- to three-mile-long "streamers" that are towed behind the ship. The recordings are enhanced, fed into a shipboard computer, and printed out as a cross section representing the structure of the earth's subsurface. Series of cross sections are combined to make illustrative maps of the underlying rock structure.

Geologists look for natural reservoirs, or "traps," in the rock formations. Structural traps occur when porous rocks fault and fold and create enormous underground hollows. Stratigraphic traps form when the density of a rock formation becomes more porous. Devices called magnetometers measure the variations in the earth's magnetic field for clues to the existence of sedimentary rock, while gravimeters detect variations in gravitational pull in order to determine density and, thus, identify porous rock, or reservoirs.

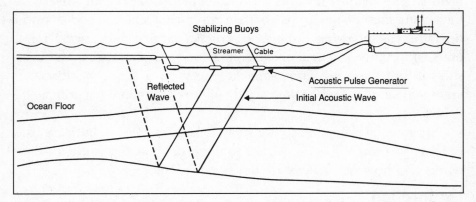

FIGURE 6   *Geophysical survey ships use acoustic pulses to map the ocean bottom in search of hidden oil reservoirs.*

Source: Joint Oil/Fisheries Committee Geophysical Manual (1986)

The results of these initial geophysical surveys, along with other information, are used by the DOI to formulate its five-year programs. The practice, in effect, allows industry to determine which areas will be leased and when.

Exploratory Drilling

Surveying gives oil companies an indication of where oil and gas might be deposited; it is no guarantee. To determine if the suspected deposits are commercially producible, exploratory wells must be drilled. These temporary holes are used for testing and sampling.

Mobile drilling rigs are brought in to drill the exploratory wells. There are three basic types.

Jack-up rig.   This is essentially a floating, bargelike hull that supports a drill rig. It is towed or self-propelled to the drill site. The rig has steel legs that are lowered to the seafloor. Elevating devices aboard the structure lift the platform on its legs above the waves. Generally, jack-ups are restricted to shallow water no more than 375 feet deep.

Semisubmersible.   A floating drill rig, the semisubmersible rides on cigar-shaped pontoons. It can be either self-propelled or towed. The rig gains stability by the partial flooding of its pontoons and legs with water. The flooding lowers the understructure into the water to a predetermined depth. The vessel is then either moored to the seabed or kept in position by motor-driven thrusters. Semisubmersibles usually operate in depths of 300 to 1,500 feet.

Drillship.   The drillship is self-propelled for great mobility. Thrusters keep it in position during drilling, or it is moored by anchor. Drilling is conducted from the deck of the ship, while various internal compartments provide crew quarters and storage space. It is the only drilling rig that can operate in waters over 1,500 feet deep.

All three types of vessels are equipped with decktop drilling derricks. The derrick supports the drilling apparatus, a drill bit attached to hollow drill pipes and rotated by a motor. The rotation of the bit against the subsea formation fractures the rock into chips.

Drillers take core samples to obtain information on the condition of the well and the type of rock. The core sample is layered like a cake. Tests conducted on the various layers of rock and mud reveal if there is any petroleum present. If there is, geologists call it a show. A show stops drilling. Geologists conduct additional tests in the open hole to measure variations in conductivity to determine the quality and quantity of oil. If the deposit is considered sizable, additional exploratory wells are sunk to delineate the field.

Exploratory drilling usually takes from sixty to ninety days. Each exploratory rig can drill approximately six wells a year. The typical exploration program drills on the average of four wells per lease.

Development and Production

Development proceeds if the company deems the oil and gas deposit economically recoverable. Most offshore fields are tapped from fixed-leg platforms, enormous steel structures that can be taller than the Empire State Building, which are attached to the ocean floor and rise above the water to support petroleum recovery equipment. Other types of production platforms—usually used in very deep waters—include tension leg platforms and guyed towers. Production systems are designed to be left in place for the fifteen to twenty years on average the wells produce.

Platforms look as though they were built from a gigantic Erector Set. The platform substructure, or "jacket," can weigh as much as 16,000 tons. It is towed to the offshore site, upended, and attached to the ocean floor by piles driven through the jacket legs. Deck sections twice the size of a football field are welded into place on top. Platform installation can take several weeks to several months. Hookup, which involves installing the necessary electrical wiring, piping, structural support, and operating equipment, takes many months more.

A platform is crammed with cranes, control rooms, living quarters, crew recreation room, helicopter landing pad, and its own power plant. Its drilling derrick towers over metal decks festooned with pipes, tanks, drums, valves, condensers, scrubbers, separators, and pumps. Steep, vertiginous stairways connect different levels. Diesel-powered motors, generators, and turbines power the equipment.

Between fifty to eighty oil and gas wells can be drilled from a single platform. Directional, or "slant," drilling allows platforms to tap wells more than 1.5 miles away and ten thousand feet below the ocean floor.

Drilling

Wells are drilled by rotating a bit with downward pressure to break up the underlying rock. The bit is attached to thirty-foot lengths of pipe that screw together. As the bit goes deeper, new lengths of drill pipe are added. The entire assembly is called a drill string. A towerlike derrick stands over the hole and is used to help lift and move the drill pipe. Bits are replaced as they become dull.

As the drilling operation progresses, the bore hole is kept full of special drilling fluids composed of clay, water, barite, and special chemicals. According to the National Academy of Sciences, many are toxic. Called mud, this material is prepared and pumped down the drill pipe through openings in the bit and back to the surface. Drilling mud serves a number of functions. It suspends and removes the cuttings from the bottom of the drill hole and carries them to the surface for removal, lubricates the drill bit, seals the wall of the well, controls pressures within the well, and helps support the weight of the drill string in the well.

Drilling takes place in stages. A surface hole is drilled first. It may range anywhere from a few hundred feet to several thousand feet deep and has a diameter of almost eighteen inches. The drill string is then pulled out and the hole is lined with hollow metal pipe, called casing, that is cemented in place. Casing is designed to prevent the hole from

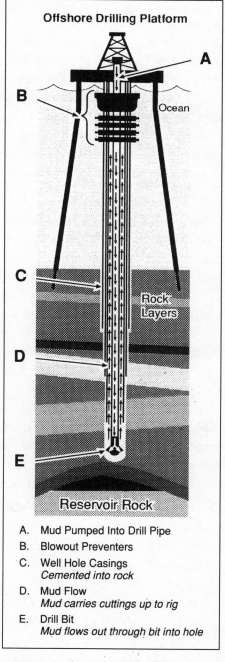

Offshore Drilling Platform

A. Mud Pumped Into Drill Pipe
B. Blowout Preventers
C. Well Hole Casings
   Cemented into rock
D. Mud Flow
   Mud carries cuttings up to rig
E. Drill Bit
   Mud flows out through bit into hole

FIGURE 7   *Diagram of offshore drilling platform.*
Source: Washington Sea Grant Program

caving in and to stop formation fluids from leaking. Next, the drill string is equipped with a bit about twelve inches around and reinserted. The hole is drilled even deeper. Again the pipe string is removed and casing is cemented into place. An eight-inch bit is reinserted to reach the final depth. This is called the bottom hole.

If the well hits petroleum, production casing is put in. A perforating gun is lowered into the hole. It contains explosive charges that are used to blast holes through the casing so that petroleum will pour in from the reservoir and flow up the well. The placement, size, and number of holes control the rate of oil flow from the well.

Treatment and Processing

Separation.   The liquid that emerges from the well is usually a mix of oil, gas, water, and sediments. This must undergo separation before the oil can be shipped to refineries. Initial separation typically takes place right on the platform.

Crude oil comes in a variety of forms and viscosities. It ranges from almost colorless to brown, green, or black. The lighter, or less viscous, the oil, the less complex the refining process. There are 3 classifications of crude: paraffin base, asphalt base, and mixed base. Crude oils that contain over 1 percent sulfur and other mineral impurities are called sour. Crude oils that have a sulfur content below 1 percent are called sweet.

Natural gas is also divided into types. It can be either "dry" or "wet." Wet gas must undergo additional treatment to remove liquids, condensable water vapors, and hydrocarbon vapors. Gas that contains hydrogen sulfide is called sour. Sour gas is odorous and, according to a report issued by the Washington Sea Grant Program, can be highly poisonous.

Offshore Storage and Treatment (OS&T).   Most oil is stored and treated onshore, but sometimes the process is carried out on converted tankers called OS&Ts. An OS&T receives crude oil emulsion from nearby platforms via subsea pipelines and processes the stream to prepare it for transportation to a refinery. The ships can store approximately 200,000 barrels of processed crude. Once processed, the oil is loaded onto tankers for shipment to onshore storage plants and refineries or sent by pipeline.

Processing.   A processing facility located onshore is like a small refinery, consisting primarily of pipes, separation and treatment tanks, and storage tanks. Separation and treatment ready the crude oil and gas stream for processing and refining by removing water, sediment, and other impurities.

Natural gas often contains corrosive and toxic hydrogen sulfide, which must be removed. Gas processing strips impurities and valuable liquefiable hydrocarbons, such as ethane, butane, and propane, from the raw gas stream before it enters the commercial gas transmission line.

Transport

Oil and gas are transported either by pipeline or tanker. Treated gas is typically piped into a local or regional gas pipeline distribution and storage system owned and operated by a gas utility company. Processed oil moves via pipelines to storage facilities and then is directed into overland pipeline systems or to a marine terminal for sea transport by tanker.

Pipelines. Pipelines are made of lengths of steel pipe that have been welded together. The exterior is coated with anticorrosives. Pipelines have a pressure source for pumping, a gathering system to bring oil and gas from one or more platforms and subsea wells to a tie-in with a larger pipe connected to shore, and facilities to maintain flow. The diameter of a pipeline depends on capacity and function. A 250,000-barrel-a-day line, for example, measures twenty-four inches in diameter.

Marine Terminals. Offshore or nearshore marine terminal facilities are used to load or unload crude oil onto vessels for the journey to refineries. Four different types of berthing and mooring arrangements are used: fixed berth, offshore pier, single buoy, and multiple buoy. Each has underwater pipelines between the berth and shore and systems to hold a tanker in position and transfer oil from tanker to shore. The loading ends are placed in water deep enough to accommodate the considerable draft of loaded tankers.

Tankers. Specially designed ships carry oil in internal cargo compartments. Millions of barrels of crude oil are transported by tanker between producing areas and refineries each day. Tankers range in size. Most of the coastal tanker traffic is made up of midsize vessels (30,000 to 80,000 deadweight tons). Supertankers (100,000 to 500,000 deadweight tons) are used for long-distance hauls. Most tankers, like the *Exxon Valdez*, have single hulls. Single hulls, according to the Washington Sea Grant Program report and numerous other studies, are more vulnerable to

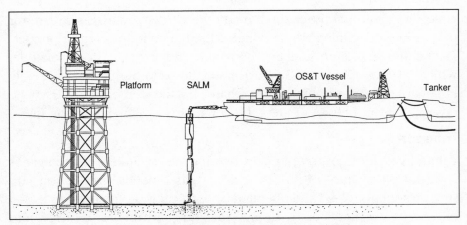

FIGURE 8   *Diagram of offshore storage and treatment ship.*
Source: Central Coast Regional Studies Program

rupture than double-hulled vessels. But so far oil companies, with few exceptions, most notably Conoco, have resisted outfitting tankers with double hulls due to costs.

Refining

Petroleum contains hydrocarbon compounds, which have a range of boiling points and various amounts of oxygen, sulfur, nitrogen, salt, water, and trace metals. It needs to be refined. Crude oil is shipped to refineries, where it is separated into natural components and blended into marketable products such as diesel fuel, lubricating oil, fuel oil, asphalt, and propane. Some crude oils and natural gas liquids are refined into petrochemical products such as toluene, benzene, and ethylene.

The typical refinery contains processing areas, storage facilities, auxiliary buildings for offices, an electrical substation, a dispensary, and a transportation system.

Shutdown

The average offshore oil and gas platform has a ten- to twenty-year life span. Once it no longer becomes profitable to continue pumping, production stops and shutdown occurs. Under current law, offshore platforms must be removed within one year after production halts. Platforms are dislodged with explosives, barged to shore, and then cut up for scrap. Divers cut the well casing off fifteen feet below the mudline and seal the well with concrete. Pipelines are left in place. Onshore facilities are typically converted to other industrial uses.

4 PEOPLE POWER

How Citizen Action Works in California

By Richard Charter

The next time you are standing on the California coast, look westward. For twenty years Californians have waged an effective campaign to block a continuing series of federal government plans that would dot the horizon with offshore oil drilling platforms. The degree of their success is best measured by what you can't see: namely, no rigs along the entire Central and Northern California coastline and a restricted number off the state's southern shores.

California's experience holds significant lessons for other states facing federal offshore drilling proposals. It shows how citizens can use the public participation opportunities made available during the lease sale process to communicate their concerns, capture media attention to enlist greater public support, and bring public opinion to bear on politicians and decision makers.

Several factors, including some fortuitous events, played a key role in the California fight. Motivation was important. While Californians' love for the beach is no secret, it took a dramatic oil spill to move people to act in the first place. Subsequent spills reinforced that urge; so did some highly unpopular actions taken by former Secretary of the Interior James Watt and his successor, Donald Hodel.

The California battle also depended on a core group of activists to keep goals focused and on sympathetic locally elected officials who responded to their needs and demands. The media coverage was also a contributing factor. By catching the media's attention in the first place and then, more importantly, holding it throughout the duration of the campaign, Californians were able to make their cause a national cause, one Washington couldn't ignore.

But of all these things, surely the most significant was Californians' willingness to believe that individuals could bring about political and social change. At heart and from the start, California's fight for coastal protection has always been a grass-roots movement. Citizen action has made the difference.

Birth of a Movement

It is no coincidence that the struggle for coastal protection from offshore oil development has its roots in California. The state has the dubious distinction of being the birthplace of offshore oil drilling. In 1896, just thirty-eight years after the first onshore oil well was drilled in Titusville, Pennsylvania, drilling took place off the coast of Summerland in Santa Barbara County. Before long, the once pristine sandy shoreline was crowded with rickety wooden piers up to 1,230 feet long, each supporting a half-dozen or more drilling rigs. Eventually some four hundred wells were punched along the stretch of beach, some pumping out oil from as deep as six hundred feet below sea level. Over the years, hundreds of other wells were drilled from piers, platforms, and artificial islands along the coast.

Prior to 1953, drilling proceeded off California's coast with little if any government control. But then technology progressed, and drilling could occur in deeper and deeper water. In order to manage the nation's offshore lands, Congress enacted the Outer Continental Shelf Lands Act (OCSLA). A system was devised for leasing offshore tracts. The first lease sale in California took place in 1963 in the waters off Santa Barbara. Fifty-seven tracts were leased and twenty wells drilled. Additional lease sales were held in the years that followed. In 1967, Phillips Petroleum's

Photo by Bob Sollen

The 1969 Santa Barbara Blowout coated 150 miles of beach in thick goo and ignited a national environmental movement.

Platform Hogan became the first oil platform to be built in federal waters off California. Three more platforms were added the following year.

Up until then, most Californians had paid little attention to offshore oil development, despite their unabashed affection for the coast. California's spectacular 1,100-mile-long coastline is an integral part of the state's identity. Nearly three out of four of the state's residents live within an hour's drive of the beach. Coastal cities are laid out so the ocean is their centerpiece. As a measure of their devotion to the coast, California's voters routinely support coastal park acquisitions by the California state park system.

But on a fateful morning in January 1969, Californians woke up to the fact that the supposedly innocuous technology of offshore drilling had a very ominous potential to create disaster. On Union Oil Company's Platform A, operating just outside state waters off the coast of Santa Barbara, a sudden surge of downhole geologic pressure triggered a huge and uncontrolled release of crude oil into the ocean. Before the "Santa Barbara Blowout" subsided, an enormous oil slick covered more than

660 square miles. At least 150 miles of formerly pristine beaches were awash in oily residue mixed with dead birds and marine animals.

In the wake of this environmental disaster, citizens in Santa Barbara began to question the safety of the other platforms operating offshore. A group of residents began meeting to discuss what they could do to protect their beloved beaches. They called themselves, appropriately enough, Get Oil Out, or GOO. With its formation, the modern-day environmental movement was born.

A Seed Is Planted

Public outrage over the Santa Barbara Blowout grew. Citizen concern forced federal OCS leasing on the California coast to come to a virtual standstill. A temporary restraint on new oil and gas leasing was also imposed in some state waters within three miles of the shoreline. Then-Interior Secretary Walter Hickel journeyed to Santa Barbara to view the disaster firsthand. In response to the public's outrage, he designated an area in the federal waters off the city of Santa Barbara as an oil and gas sanctuary.

The creation of the "Hickel Preserve" was nothing more than a token gesture, of course, but it did plant a seed—a seed that has grown into a nationwide movement in support of a bill that would create a permanent ocean sanctuary for most of the nation's outer continental shelf.

The public frustration over the blowout needed a political outlet. As the 1970s began, there was also a rapidly growing concern throughout California over the pace of commercial and residential development along the coast. In a move to preserve the coast, voters passed a ballot measure in 1972, the California Coastal Initiative. The initiative led to the passage of the California Coastal Act, which established a permanent commission to administer land-use and general growth management controls along the strip of land along the shore known as the coastal zone. By passing a state coastal law, California gained authority under the federal Coastal Zone Management Act to review federal offshore drilling plans to make sure they were consistent with the state's own coastal zone management efforts. The state has relied on this authority to restrict drilling.

In 1973, a new energy crisis developed—the OPEC oil embargo. Concern over the nation's energy security compelled Congress to break the stalemate over new domestic offshore drilling. A congressional committee formulated amendments to OCSLA to allow OCS leasing while guaranteeing environmental protection. The amendments also gave coastal states and their governors more of a direct role in leasing decisions.

While the amendments were simple in concept, they proved difficult to enact into law. By the time the bill finally achieved passage in 1978, congressional supporters of the oil industry had seriously eroded many of its key environmental protection measures. The resulting legislation was an improvement, but it did not resolve the conflict brewing off the California coast.

Let's Make a Deal

The OCSLA amendments were put to the test shortly after their passage. In 1978 President Jimmy Carter announced plans to proceed with a Central and Northern California offshore drilling proposal, known as Lease Sale Number 53. It targeted a series of five undersea geologic structures or basins.

The president's plan alarmed local government officials in California. A Santa Cruz county supervisor, Gary Patton, perceived the sale as a threat to his county's clean air, unpolluted coastline, and growing tourism industry. Patton launched an information campaign, sending two- and three-page action alerts about the drilling plan to other elected officials serving in the region targeted by the sale. They decided to join forces, forming a Local Government Coordination Program to keep themselves abreast of federal drilling decisions.

Today, eight coastal counties and seventeen coastal cities fund the program with a modest $99,540 annual budget. The Local Government Coordination Program, with its full-time coordinator/advocate, keeps local officials informed about what they need to do. By institutionalizing their concern and funding an ongoing effort, local governments took a critically important step that made possible the mobilization of both citizen and government action in a timely and effective way. This particular program has been highly instrumental in making the California success story possible.

Citizens from various coastal communities were motivated to form their own grass-roots groups to complement government action. People

Institutionalizing Local Government Concern

California provides three examples of programs started by local govern-ments to formalize their involvement in the offshore oil leasing decision-making process. The earliest coalition, the Local Government Coordination Program (LGCP), was formed in the early 1980s to keep several coastal county boards of supervisors up to date about federal drilling proposals. The participating county governments pool money allocated from their general funds to support the program. As other information programs were established, the LGCP evolved into a federal lobbying arm for the counties and, later, coastal cities.

The next formal local government group, the Oil Information Program of Save Our Shores, was established by the city of Santa Cruz in 1986. Working with the local citizen group Save Our Shores, the program promotes local government ordinances regulating onshore facilities for offshore oil and increased safety measures for oil tanker traffic. Financial support comes primarily from coastal cities up and down the state. Largely as a result of this program, a third of the local coastal jurisdictions in California have passed ordinances regulating onshore oil facilities. The program heavily emphasizes public education. It makes available speakers, slide shows, and other multimedia presentations.

In June 1987, six central California counties took advantage of a special state program that funnels revenues generated from federal offshore oil leases paid to the state to local jurisdictions. The counties of Monterey, Santa Cruz, San Mateo, San Francisco, Marin, and Sonoma created the Central Coast Regional Studies Program to hire a full-time professional staff charged with studying the potential impacts of offshore oil drilling proposed by the federal government in Central California.

The Regional Studies Program has six areas of interest for specific study: air quality, scenario development, technical review, oil spill planning, socioeconomic impacts, and public participation. The program has awarded a series of contracts paid for by the special state offshore oil lease revenue-sharing program to independent consultants to complete work on each of the elements. The products include technical reports, presentations by offshore oil and environmental experts, resource mapping, periodic updates, and public briefings.

While much of the work is oriented toward planners and local government officials, a large emphasis is placed on public involvement in the federal lease sale process. All reports produced by the program are summarized for general public distribution. Updates are regularly disseminated to keep the public informed about the lease sale process.

with a variety of different interests joined. Commercial fishermen saw drilling rigs as a direct threat to their livelihood. Local business owners worried that the resulting industrialization from offshore oil development would jeopardize their tourism-based economy. And coastal residents saw the daily pollutants from drilling and the potential environmental disaster of a spill as threats to the quality of life.

One citizen group, for instance, was called Friends of the Coast. It succeeded in attracting additional supporters by distributing flyers that had been printed for free by a sympathetic printer. Fund-raisers were held to raise money for a growing mailing list and newsletter distribution. Celebrations held in local coastal redwood groves complete with blue-grass music and potluck meals helped attract even more supporters. A steering committee was established. It had only two rules: to have fun in the process of educating the public about offshore drilling dangers and to conduct business meetings on the beach whenever possible.

Out of these various groups evolved what became known as the OCS Environmental Coalition. Meeting monthly or bimonthly, the coalition served as an information-sharing tool. It kept participating groups continually attuned to new developments in the fast-moving political arena so that all would be aware of how best to contribute to the common goal of protecting the coast. Eventually, the coalition grew to include member organizations from nearly every coastal state in the country. It began holding annual strategy meetings in Washington, DC, to coordinate the fight against OCS leasing plans on a national scale and to further the cause of permanent ocean protection everywhere.

The formation of these groups was noticed by Washington. President Carter's Secretary of the Interior, Cecil Andrus, decided to create a way in which these various interest groups could participate in the decision-making process. His plan did not envision participation to the degree of having veto authority but only to the point of allowing local interests to help decide where and when drilling could proceed. The idea was to hold informational meetings for elected officials and interested members of the public. A series of meetings to be presided over by officials from the regional office of the DOI were scheduled for California.

As the specific details of Lease Sale Number 53 became apparent, local officials turned up the pressure on their congressional representatives. Governor Edmund G. "Jerry" Brown took a strong personal interest in the issue and arranged a meeting with Andrus. He invited a number

Huge public rallies staged by grassroots activists in California generated extensive national media attention.

of different interest groups to attend. Theirs was a single voice: adamant opposition to the lease sale plan.

As the meeting concluded, Andrus acknowledged their opposition by announcing that he was inclined to drop the four northern basins of the proposed lease sale while keeping the southern one. He said he would go ahead and hold public hearings on the drilling plan during the following summer and make his decision in the fall of 1980 based on the information and testimony presented at the hearings.

The public hearings process was given new significance by the secretary's commitment to focus on the results of the testimony. Local governments and coastal environmental groups viewed the hearings as opportunities to develop, at little or no financial cost, a much broader and more educated constituency. The resulting public participation presented an ideal way to utilize the media to broadcast the nature of the threat to the coast among the general populace. It was, at the outset, a monumental task to convince two or three hundred people to have enough faith in the process to get up and speak in front of cameras and a crowd. A tremendous amount of organizing was dedicated to assuring a strong turnout for the public hearings.

The citizen activists went to work. Shared mailing lists from preexisting conservation groups were used for mass mailings. Free advance training sessions were conducted in many communities to help people gain the self-confidence to get up and speak in public. Newsletters and action alerts were produced and distributed.

By the time the hearings were held, the organizers were ready. People lined up to testify. The first to speak were elected officials. The strategy here was to take advantage of television's method of covering news events. TV crews tend to shoot the first half hour of a meeting, then rush back to the station to edit their tape. By filling the footage to be aired on the evening news with noteworthy elected officials, activists turned an environmental issue into a political issue.

The size of the public turnout also attracted media attention. The crowds swelled with every hearing. The speakers were polite, passionate, and adamant. The hearings encompassed laughter, tears, poetry, scientific research, irate fishermen, oiled dead birds, and singing grade schoolers. The message was clear. Californians loved their coast and did not want it dotted with drilling rigs and oil spills. A dramatic shift suddenly occurred in the control over the message that was going out over the airwaves. It passed from Interior's hands to the public's. And the audience for that message also shifted. No longer was it being heard just by the officials holding the hearings. Politicians everywhere heard it, including those in Washington. During this time a presidential campaign was under way. The environment became a major platform plank. On October 16, 1980, true to the promise made by Secretary Andrus, President Carter announced that he was deleting the four northern basins from consideration for leasing as part of Lease Sale Number 53. Banner headlines of the presidential reprieve for the coast ran on the front page of California newspapers and opened the evening news. A workable compromise had been reached. Californians thought the coast was saved.

Let's Break a Deal, Part 1

The rescue was short-lived, however, because the very next month Ronald Reagan defeated Jimmy Carter at the polls. The new president appointed James Watt as his Secretary of the Interior. Three weeks after he was confirmed, Watt reversed the Carter decision on Lease Sale

Number 53. Not only were the four northern basins back in the plan, but the lease sale itself was imminent.

Watt's announcement couldn't have backfired more. It served as a call to arms to many Californians who may not have otherwise physically joined the fight against coastal drilling. Californian's congressional delegation was also angered by Watt's decision. Members immediately hatched a plan to reel in his scheme.

Their strategy was simple: tie his hands by cutting off his budget. This is the way it worked: Funding for the Interior Department is approved on a yearly basis through budgetary action by the House and Senate Appropriations Committees. The power of this particular committee process lies in its detailed "line-item" decision-making capability. Federal projects and proposals live and die according to whether or not they are granted funding. No funding means no spending. The yearly budget for the Interior Department must be approved project by project as it originates in the House and Senate Subcommittees on Interior.

When the fiscal year 1982 funding for the OCS leasing program at the Department of the Interior came up for discussion, a minor technical amendment to the language in the bill was added by California representatives. It said that since key scientific studies necessary to evaluate the impacts of leasing had not been completed by the Interior Department, a temporary one-year delay was necessary. In essence, this language prohibited Interior from spending funds to lease the four northern basins of Lease Sale Number 53 during the next fiscal year.

With this deft political move, the concept of the Congressional "OCS moratorium" was born. It was to become the prototype for nearly a decade of congressional intervention in drilling plans for the California coast. Eventually, the moratorium would also be extended to include other environmentally sensitive areas around the country.

In the years that followed, the moratorium scenario was repeated. Each year, the Interior Department would request funding for a new OCS leasing proposal. Each year, California citizens and their elected officials would press for a new moratorium. The moratorium usually passed by only a one-vote margin. Through fiscal years 1982, 1983, 1984, and 1985, a California moratorium was renewed, first for Northern and Central California, and later for Southern California tracts as well. Through similar cooperative efforts, the Georges Bank fishery off New England obtained a similar yearly moratorium.

Despite the moratorium's success, there was always the underlying concern that eventually the House Appropriations Committee might lose patience with the yearly OCS moratorium effort. This fear was a valid concern, because the margin of the vote in the full Appropriations Committee was just too close each year to be considered reliable. The oil industry knew that the outcome was close and spent countless hours and untold dollars trying to pressure key votes on this committee. If the moratorium were to lapse for even a single year, drilling would commence and the coast would be lost.

Let's Break a Deal, Part 2

Due in part to his unpopular offshore oil drilling policies, Watt was forced to resign in 1985. His successor was Donald Hodel, Watt's deputy during the formulation of his aggressive five-year OCS leasing program. Hodel tried a new tactic of trying to negotiate a deal with the key players in the moratorium process. He broached the idea of pursuing a compromise settlement with the California congressional representatives that spring.

Photo by Brad Matsen, National Fisherman Magazine

California's fishermen have played an important role in the fight against offshore oil drilling.

Because everything Congress undertakes revolves around compromise of some kind, many in the House felt that a negotiated solution that resolved the OCS issue and lent some predictability to the future of the California coast was preferable to the risk of saving the coast one year at a time.

Hodel produced a detailed series of maps of the OCS tracts off the entire California coastline indicating where the oil industry most wanted to explore for oil and gas. The idea behind the negotiated agreement was to open some portion of the high-interest tracts to leasing, exploration, and subsequent development in exchange for placing the remaining tracts off limits until the year 2000.

Secretary Hodel wanted a minimum of two hundred tracts. The California delegation could come up with only about a hundred tracts that it deemed to be expendable. Eventually a compromise was reached on 150 tracts.

Despite the ongoing negotiations, the House Appropriations Committee continued to prepare for a vote on the fiscal year 1986 congressional moratorium. On the eve of a key committee vote, Hodel called California representatives to his office at the Interior Department for one final negotiating session. A document was prepared by Hodel's staff that outlined the terms of a compromise agreement based on the prompt leasing of 150 tracts.

The deal was struck and the long fight appeared to be over. A joint press conference was held by the majority of the California congressional delegation and Interior Secretary Hodel. The terms and conditions of the agreement were explained to the press in detail. The negotiating process was extolled as an example of conflict resolution at its finest. Later that same day, the full House Appropriations Committee dropped the California moratorium from the text of the Interior bill. Grass-roots activists, however, were dissatisfied with the compromise.

Their fears proved correct. During the August congressional recess, Secretary Hodel suddenly announced that the deal was off. There would be no ban on drilling, he said. It seems the tracts selected for drilling did not contain enough oil and gas to interest the oil companies, he explained, but the ones excluded by the compromise did.

Just as Watt's announcement had, Hodel's decision triggered an enormous backlash. It was as if a state of emergency had been declared in California's coastal communities. Citizens and local officials immediately set about formulating new and creative approaches to stop drilling.

One idea was to utilize the electoral process to assert strong local land use controls over onshore OCS facilities. In Santa Cruz, a ballot measure that gave citizens the right to vote on coastal land use zoning changes that would accommodate construction of any onshore industrial facility associated with offshore drilling was put before voters. The measure, called the Onshore Facilities Ordinance, passed by a margin of 82 percent. It allowed the city government to help fund a local government coalition on OCS issues. Funds provided by the city of Santa Cruz helped create an ambitious and hugely successful outreach program. The tactic of requiring a vote for onshore facilities spread to other jurisdictions. By 1990, a total of twenty-three more such measures had been enacted at the city and county levels along the California coast.

Meanwhile, in Washington, Congress again reinstated the OCS moratorium for California waters through the Interior appropriations bill. This time, the 1987 moratorium contained the equivalent of a two-year ban on funding for the California lease sales.

At the state level, the California legislature adopted a joint resolution of both the Assembly and the State Senate—a measure called AJR 91—which called upon Congress to provide permanent protection for the entire Central and Northern California coast. This eventually led to the introduction of a bill called the California Ocean Sanctuary Act, which was introduced by California Representative Barbara Boxer. It called for the enactment of a permanent prohibition on new offshore drilling, ocean minerals mining, toxic waste incineration, and toxic dumping within all unleased federal waters off the entire California coast.

Finally, the seed planted with the creation of the Hickel Preserve back in the days following the Santa Barbara Blowout began to sprout. The idea of an ocean sanctuary was embraced at the grass-roots level, and virtually all of the efforts of various citizen groups now went into generating public awareness and support. Citizen organizers began a letter-writing campaign to help enlist congressional sponsors for the legislation. The 1988 presidential race was heating up, and supporters began pressing candidates on the issue. They saw the election of an administration sympathetic to ocean sanctuary as key to changing the federal OCS leasing program once and for all.

Taking Public Hearings to New Heights

Meanwhile, citizen groups returned to the lease sale public participation process as a way to halt the government's immediate drilling plans. In 1987 a new five-year plan went into effect. It called for five new lease sales off California. The Department of the Interior scheduled two public hearings in February 1988 on the first new sale—Lease Sale Number 91 drilling plan for Northern California. Sale Number 91 encompassed over a million offshore acres along the coast of Mendocino and Humboldt counties and included some of the same tracts that had been part of the original Sale Number 53. The first public hearing was to be held on the coast of Humboldt County in Eureka. The second hearing, two days later, would be held in the rural village of Fort Bragg on the Mendocino coast.

Mendocino County was the birthplace of the ocean sanctuary movement, and when word got out that the DOI was coming to town to find out what the community thought about offshore drilling, citizens sprang into action.

Volunteers began working to enhance the turnout at these hearings. The effort resembled a high-budget campaign run by a major Madison Avenue advertising agency, but without the big budget. The process of getting the word out involved posters, print ads, radio spots, and the distribution of a hundred thousand tabloid newsprint flyers. Extensive coverage in the local press triggered word-of-mouth discussion over coffee shop breakfasts, radio channels at sea, and backyard fences.

The DOI made its first stop in Eureka. Historically, attendance for similar drilling hearings had always been small in Eureka, but not this time. The public turnout marked the beginning of a new phase in the controversy over drilling. There seemed to be an endless parade of people pouring into the hearing room. The crowd quickly overflowed outside.

The hearing in the Mendocino County town of Fort Bragg was even more heavily attended. Every seat in the hearing hall was filled. It was standing room only, and the waiting line to get into the hall stretched down the steps and around the corner of the building into the street.

Elected officials presented their testimony first. Congressional representatives, state senators and assemblymen, and the state attorney general joined local county supervisors and mayors in decrying the lease sale proposal. Statements from 1988 Democratic presidential candidates

Photo by Rick Dullea, Coastal Concern, Marin

California Congressman Leon Panetta exemplifies the willingness of elected officials to go on record in opposition to federal drilling plans and has been a key factor in California's effort to protect its coast.

supporting protection of the coast were read into the record.

Then it was time for ordinary citizens to speak. The hearing testimony came in waves. Emotional, musical, poetic, and artistic presentations were intermixed with rigid technical testimony about the hazards drilling rigs pose to the marine environment. Dancers, painters, fishermen, schoolchildren, young and old—all walked up to the microphone. The speeches were intense and from the heart. Outside the hall, the entire street was filled with people waiting for a chance to get inside and testify on behalf of their coastline.

The hearing lasted for two days. More than a thousand people spoke. The event made headlines around the country, and coverage was broadcast on prime time network news.

The drilling controversy was now firmly a part of the 1988 presidential election. Millions of Americans knew about the Fort Bragg hearing. Congress heard about it. In other coastal states facing similar OCS proposals, Fort Bragg became a legend. As the June 1988 California primary approached, even former oilman George Bush had to take a position on the issue. Two days prior to the California primary, Bush said that, if elected, he would be inclined to postpone Northern California Lease Sale Number 91 until it could be reevaluated.

How to Build Your Own Ocean Protection Movement

- **Play the government's "game," but play it your way.** Utilize the bureaucratic processes to get your own message out. Don't be tempted to refuse to respond to a written comment period or participate in a public hearing for fear of being co-opted. Use the process to advance your own goals.

- **Help the media.** Be exceptionally forbearing and patient with your press contacts. They are your conduit to the general public.

- **Have your "ducks" lined up.** When the media spotlight focuses on your issue, be ready to present your facts and point of view. Be clear and concise with your message. Have your scientific data at hand and be accurate, so that you will develop a reputation as a reliable news-making source.

- **Be patient.** Building a grass-roots movement takes time and can be a slow and cumulative process.

- **Timing is everything.** Harvest public outrage over your issue when it is at a peak. Don't wear people out with too many meetings.

- **Write letters.** Writing letters works. Paying the price of a stamp and committing the few minutes it takes to write to a member of Congress can be the most important actions an individual can take. Generate faith in this process at the grass-roots level. You cannot prevail without it.

- **Cooperate with your elected officials.** Develop an open line of communication with your elected officials at the local, state, and federal levels. Get to know your congressional representatives and develop mutual trust with them. Monitor their actions to make sure that they are working actively to achieve your goals.

The Movement Goes National

The coastal protection movement in California became part of mainstream politics. Offshore drilling provided one of the key issues by which candidates for any office were measured. California activists became increasingly aware that parallel movements were beginning to make major strides in other coastal states threatened by similar drilling plans. In Florida, a proposal to bring offshore drilling to the southeastern part of the state and the Keys had aroused strong public outcry. North Carolina, New Jersey, New England, Alaska, and just about every other state with a coastline had been undergoing similar organizational efforts.

- **Convince local government to institutionalize its concern.** It is necessary to get your local government to allocate funds for OCS-issue coordinating programs and outreach programs. Full-time advocates are essential.

- **Keep your message before the public.** But also allow intermittent periods in which the media and the citizenry are able to "rest" from your message as well. Think of developing an issue as similar to conducting a musical score. Quiet periods highlight the times of heightened activity.

- **Always print more literature than you think you will need.** "Saturation" media will almost always give you the turnout you need, but your response will be only a percentage of the brochures you distribute.

- **Use your imagination freely to make news.** It has to be real news, however. Free press coverage can do more to influence public opinion than perhaps any other factor. You will not need to purchase expensive advertising space if a colorful event can get the same exposure without cost. There is an increased level of credibility gained from appearing in the news pages.

- **Have fun.** Don't allow your personal happiness to hinge on the outcome of any political issue. Think of the bureaucratic process as a giant Monopoly game. Play it as best you can, pass Go, buy hotels and houses, and collect penalties from other players. Be a good sport. If you keep a sense of detachment, your effectiveness will soar. Recharge whenever you can. You can't heal the planet unless you heal yourself. Spend time on your favorite beach or at other natural cathedrals. The earth and the ocean will give you strength.

The combined efforts of James Watt and Donald Hodel had triggered a backlash that now reached from ocean to ocean. Any legislative effort aimed at achieving a long-term resolution through congressional action would need to occur in the context of a nationwide grass-roots movement.

George Bush prevailed in the November 1988 presidential race. During his first budget address to Congress, the president recalled his commitment to California voters on offshore drilling and announced he would temporarily postpone three of the most controversial sales— Northern California Lease Sale Number 91 and Southern California Lease

Sale Number 95, as well as Southeast Florida Sale Number 116. He also announced that he was creating a Cabinet-level OCS task force to conduct a thorough, year-long study of the issues surrounding these three specific lease sales. While reiterating his support for expanded offshore drilling, Bush said that it should go forward only where it could be demonstrated to be compatible with protection of the environment.

California Lease Sales Number 91 and Number 95 and Florida Sale Number 116 were placed on hold while the president's OCS task force convened. One of its first acts was to hold a series of public hearings in various California and Florida communities. The overwhelming theme of the public testimony presented at these hearings focused on the need for permanent protection of all proposed lease sale areas from drilling. A secondary theme was the need for a new national energy policy that emphasized conservation and clean energy alternatives. Massive demonstrations accompanied each of the hearings, with ocean sanctuary signs, speakers, and extensive television coverage.

The next event to influence the fight against offshore oil drilling took place on March 24, 1989. The *Exxon Valdez* ripped open its cargo tanks on Bligh Reef, Alaska, and in its wake, the environmental danger of oil development became etched in the minds of Americans forever.

At that time the Subcommittee on Interior Appropriations had already held its initial hearings to consider a renewed OCS moratorium for fiscal year 1990. Suddenly, it seemed that almost every coastal state threatened with new offshore drilling plans now wanted a moratorium, too.

The configuration of the fiscal 1990 moratorium encompassed a one-year prohibition on all new leasing off California, including a prohibition on pre-lease planning steps. In addition, the moratorium included a ban that precluded new drilling on active leases off the west coast of Florida and a similar ban on exploring active leases in Alaska's fishery-rich Bristol Bay. A prohibition on leasing off the mid-Atlantic region, extending from Maryland to the Connecticut-Rhode Island border, was added as well. The ongoing moratorium for New England's Georges Bank fishing grounds was extended. Over sixty thousand letters in support of the moratorium flowed in to Congress from around the nation.

As the crucial vote before the full House Appropriations Committee approached, it was apparent that this was going to be a difficult vote. In spite of the strong support from so many state delegations, the geographic scope of the protection was more extensive than anything attempted in previous years. But on the weekend immediately prior to the vote in the full committee, three major oil spills occurred almost simultaneously around the nation: in the Houston ship channel, in the Delaware River, and off the coast of Rhode Island. Partially as a result of the public outrage over these spills, the full OCS moratorium survived the Appropriations Committee intact, achieved final passage in the Congress, and was signed into law by President Bush.

Late in the summer of 1989, a draft report compiling the work of the president's OCS task force was printed and distributed. The draft report contained only a compendium of the range of viewpoints presented during the 1989 task force hearings. The possibilities listed in the report ranged from proceeding immediately with leasing and drilling to delaying leasing for an interim period. In November 1989, a National Academy of Sciences panel, which had been asked by the OCS task force to analyze the available scientific data, issued the results of its own investigation. The report concluded that the Interior Department did not have adequate scientific information to allow drilling to proceed and assure that the environment would be protected.

The president's OCS task force was scheduled to make its final recommendations to President Bush at the beginning of January 1990. The final report of the task force was transmitted to Bush in the form of a single copy, which the president kept secret. A leaked copy of the document obtained by the press indicated that the completed report did not contain any recommendation for permanent protection. In January 1990, a bipartisan letter, signed by the majority of the California congressional delegation, was sent to the president. The letter asked Bush to provide permanent protection for the areas studied by the task force and extend it to the equally sensitive central California Lease Sale Number 119 as well. A second letter endorsing permanent protection was sent to the president, signed by the entire Florida delegation.

In November 1989, California Representative Barbara Boxer introduced an expanded version of her first bill, the Ocean Protection Act of 1990. Congresswoman Boxer was joined by over sixty bipartisan cosponsors representing every coastal state. The Ocean Protection Act would create a zone of permanent protection around the continental United States and Alaska. The Gulf of Mexico, where extensive leasing had already occurred, was not included because of a lack of support from congressional representatives from that region. The act held the promise of eventually replacing the year-by-year moratorium with permanent protection on a national scale.

On June 26, 1990, President Bush finally made public his response to the task force's report on the one Florida and the two California lease sales. Basically, he canceled the three lease sales and announced his intention to delay drilling off California, Washington-Oregon, southwest Florida, and Georges Bank in New England until the year 2000. Despite the president's call for a ten-year delay, the fight for protection of the nation's coastline is far from over. Californians, now joined by coastal activists from around the country, will continue their grass-roots efforts. They are following the strategy that has served them so well: using the public participation process to the fullest extent possible. While much has changed in this two-decade-old struggle, their goal remains the same: the permanent protection of the state's valuable coastline.

5 NEW HORIZONS

How Energy Alternatives Can Replace Offshore Drilling

Ever since the OPEC oil embargo of 1973, the nation's energy program has sought to reduce dependency on foreign oil in order to increase national security. This is a key justification for the continued leasing of the country's OCS despite the known environmental and socioeconomic risks. The fact is, offshore oil drilling can only be a short-term solution to the nation's energy needs. The total amount of undiscovered OCS oil and gas resources, including central and western Gulf of Mexico, is estimated to be only 21.4 billion barrels, or enough energy equivalent to fuel the nation for about 1,300 days at the current rate of consumption, which is roughly 17 million barrels per day.

Including OCS oil and gas with domestic onshore reserves won't make the nation energy self-sufficient. Undiscovered resources amount to only 81.5 billion barrels of oil and gas, or a fraction of the remaining petroleum in the whole world. Yet we consume 6.2 billion barrels each year, roughly half of which is imported. As long as the country is dependent on oil, it will remain dependent on foreign sources.

Even the oil industry concedes this. In a *Washington Post* advertisement, Mobil Oil editorialized, "The bulk of the world's oil reserves is in the Middle East. But that's a factor of geology, not politics. It's also geologically true that this country will never again be self-sufficient in oil. Imports are inevitable, but so long as normal trade relations exist, it hardly matters whether the import level is 10 percent, 40 percent, or 60 percent. Japan imports virtually all its oil, and the Japanese economy doesn't seem any the worse for it."

There are much more environmentally prudent and cost-effective ways to add to the nation's strategic energy reserves than drilling offshore. We need to tell the government to develop alternative energy sources, practice energy efficiency, and squeeze more oil out of already existing developed fields.

Many industrial countries with little or no domestic oil reserves have made energy efficiency a cornerstone of their national energy policy. In fact, *Scientific American* reports that if the United States were as energy efficient as Japan, it could slash $220 billion off the nation's energy bill each year.

Energy Efficiency

The technology exists today to make automobiles, buildings, and factories that use half the current amount of energy. By raising automobile gas mileage standards, weatherizing houses and other buildings, expanding mass transit, and using more efficient light bulbs and appliances, the nation can save the equivalent of about 45 billion barrels of oil by the year 2020. Energy efficiency operates under the same principle as Benjamin Franklin's homily: A penny saved *is* a penny earned.

Energy efficiency is nothing new. It got a false start following the 1973 oil embargo. When OPEC pulled the plug on cheap fuel, Congress reacted by encouraging energy conservation, along with the development of such alternatives as solar energy, ocean power, and synthetic fuels. At one point in 1979, energy legislation was pending before seventy-eight committees and subcommittees in the House of Representatives.

Little, however, resulted. During the Reagan administration, the government made a wholesale retreat from supporting alternative forms of energy. The withdrawal is best measured in dollars. Between 1981 and

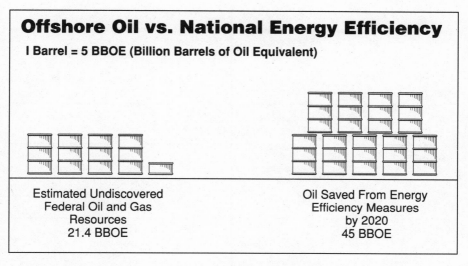

Offshore Oil vs. National Energy Efficiency

I Barrel = 5 BBOE (Billion Barrels of Oil Equivalent)

| Estimated Undiscovered Federal Oil and Gas Resources 21.4 BBOE | Oil Saved From Energy Efficiency Measures by 2020 45 BBOE |

FIGURE 9 *The amount of oil that could be obtained through energy efficiency programs greatly exceeds the nation's estimated undiscovered offshore resources.*
Source: NRDC

1987, for example, the Department of Energy's budget for conservation and technological development of alternative energy sources was slashed from $292.5 million to $71.2 million. The 76 percent drop in financial support for small hydropower, wind power, solar electricity, geothermal energy, and the like cost the country potential major savings in energy conservation. As a result, by the mid-1980s alternative energy resources met, at most, 3 percent of U.S. energy needs.

Gas Mileage Standards

The single most glaring example of how the federal government backed away from energy efficiency involves gas mileage standards. The transportation sector is the biggest consumer of oil in the country, commanding nearly four billion barrels of oil a year, or more than 60 percent of the nation's annual fuel requirements. Increasing gas mileage standards for cars and light trucks, which make up three-quarters of the transportation sector, would cut this amount by over one-fourth.

Fuel-efficient cars are no pipe dream. In her book on future fuel economy innovation in automobiles, Deborah Bleviss singles out a Renault that gets 100 miles per gallon in the city and 146 mpg on the

FUEL-EFFICIENT PROTOTYPES

	Model	Fuel Economy	Maximum # of Passengers	Innovative Features
General Motors	TPC	61 mpg city 74 mpg highway	2	Aluminum body and engine.
Ford	(no name)	57 mpg city 92 mpg highway	5	Advanced diesel engine.
Volkswagen	Auto 2000	63 mpg city 71 mpg highway	5	Advanced diesel engine. High use of plastic and aluminum. Improved aerodynamics. Flywheel energy storage.
Volkswagen	VW-E80	74 mpg city 99 mpg highway	4	High use of plastic and aluminum. Flywheel energy storage
Volvo	LCP 2000	63 mpg city 81 mpg highway	4	Advanced diesel engine. High use of magnesium. Improved aerodynamics.
Renault	EVE+	63 mpg city 81 mpg highway	5	Advanced diesel engine. Improved aerodynamics.
Renault	VESTA2	78 mpg city 107 mpg highway	4	High use of light material. Highly improved aerodynmaics.

FUEL-EFFICIENT PROTOTYPES UNDER DEVELOPMENT

	Model	Fuel Economy	Maximum # of Passengers	Innovative Features
Peugeot	VERA+	55 mpg city 87 mpg highway	5	Advanced diesel engine. High use of light material. Improved aerodynamics.
Peugeot	ECO 2000	70 mpg city 77 mpg highway	4	High use of light material. Improved aerodymanics.
Toyota	AXV	89 mpg city 110 mpg highway	5	Advanced diesel engine. Continuously variable transmission. High use of plastic and aluminum. Improved aerodynamics.

FIGURE 10 *Increasing gas mileage standards in cars and light trucks will create an enormous "conservation oil field." Many fuel-efficient prototypes are currently being tested. When will these cars hit the road?*
Source: *Technology Review*

highway. She also reports on the Volvo LCP, a two- to four-passenger vehicle that gets 63 mpg in the city and 81 mpg on the highway. Now ready for mass production, it is estimated to cost no more to produce than a standard subcompact.

Despite these technological possibilities, American automobile manufacturers have persuaded the federal government to roll back gas mileage standards rather than increase them every year from 1986 through 1990. The decision to lower the mileage requirement from 27.5 mpg to 26 mpg for 1986, 1987, and 1988 model year cars will waste 150 million barrels of oil over the life of those fleets. Lower mileage standards for the 1989 and 1990 fleets will squander an additional 80 million barrels. To put this amount in perspective, the DOI estimates that the offshore area from North Carolina to Florida will produce roughly 230 million barrels of oil equivalent. By rolling back automobile efficiency standards, the government is pouring nearly the same amount of oil that lies off the south Atlantic coast down the drain.

The government's decision to lower gas mileage standards does more than burn oil needlessly. It sanctions pollution. Lowering the standards just for the 1989 and 1990 fleets will pump an additional 17 million tons of carbon dioxide emissions into the atmosphere. CO_2 is one of the main greenhouse gases, which are responsible for global warming.

There are other ways to stifle the guzzling of oil by the transportation sector. Expanding the nation's mass transit system and increasing ridership will produce major savings. Mass transit is more fuel efficient than automobiles and results in less automobile travel miles in areas well served by mass transit. A 50 percent increase in transit ridership over current levels could save more than three billion barrels of oil over the next twenty years. That is more than three times the amount of oil equivalent that the DOI estimates lies between Canada and Miami.

Weatherizing Houses and Other Buildings

Aggressive home insulation programs could also swell the conservation oil field. Efficiency improvements in the home save mainly natural gas, but natural gas can be used instead of oil in industry and to heat people's homes and water. The replaced oil can then be used in the transportation sector, which is almost completely dependent on petroleum for its energy needs. If homes were fully insulated and used the most efficient furnaces and water heaters available today, the United States could save the equivalent of almost 16 billion barrels of oil by 2020, more than the identified OCS resources for the entire nation. Pilot programs sponsored by utilities and reported by the Oak Ridge National Laboratory show that almost 90 percent of the potential savings can be achieved within a three-year implementation period, as compared with the ten- to fifteen-year period needed to realize production from offshore oil discoveries.

An effective way to save oil is to refit single-pane windows with high-technology, highly insulated ones. Windows, according to *Scientific American,* leak about a third of the heat out of U.S. homes. Highly insulated windows—typically, two panes of glass with a very thin sheet of Mylar and argon gas between them—limit heat loss significantly. A study conducted by the Rocky Mountain Institute and reported by the *New York Times* demonstrates that if windows like these were installed nationwide, they would save more energy than is contained in the oil that flows through the Trans-Alaska Pipeline System.

Lighting

New lighting fixtures also save oil. High-efficiency fluorescent bulbs burn about one-fourth the kilowatt-hours of traditional bulbs. This means that

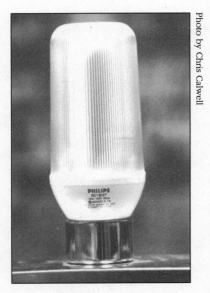

Photo by Chris Calwell

if you were to replace a single 60-watt light bulb burning 24 hours a day with a 16-watt compact fluorescent bulb, you would save 385 kilowatt-hours a year, or three-fifths of a barrel of oil. According to the *New York Times*, an estimated one billion light sockets in the United States could accommodate high-efficiency bulbs for an equivalent savings of 600 million barrels of oil.

Refitting office buildings with improved troffers—the typically four-foot-long inverted troughs on office and factory ceilings used to hold four fluorescent tubes and a ballast—also saves oil. In traditional troffers, the tubes are 40 watts each and the ballast is 40 watts, for a total load of 200

Replacing a 75-watt incandescent bulb with this 18-watt compact fluorescent light bulb will save a barrel of oil.

watts. But by using bulbs of a slightly improved design and installing a mirrorlike reflector behind them, the same lighting job can be done for 80 watts. In areas where electricity is generated by oil-fueled power plants, the *New York Times* reports, replacing a troffer that runs twelve hours a day, five days a week with a model that uses 120 watts less would save more than half a barrel of oil a year.

Appliance Efficiency

Close to one-third of the energy consumed in buildings goes to power such major home electrical appliances as refrigerators, freezers, water heaters, and air conditioners. It takes the equivalent of almost 4.4 million barrels of oil a day to run them; that accounts for 12 percent of the nation's energy budget, says *Scientific American.*

Much of that energy could be saved through tougher appliance efficiency standards. Some progress has already been made along this line. Consider the refrigerator, for example. It has been the largest single electricity user in most American homes. In 1977, the typical 16- to 18-cubic-foot, automatic-defrost refrigerator consumed 1,900 kilowatt-hours per year. But by using better insulation, compressors, and gaskets, it is possible to cut its energy demand by nearly two-thirds. Such improvements add less than $150 to the retail cost and are paid back in energy savings in less than one year.

These savings are now being realized due to new mandatory national standards. By 1993, the standard for refrigerator electricity consumption should reach 700 kilowatt-hours per year. According to *Scientific American,* for the 125 million refrigerators and freezers in the United States, the energy saving will be equivalent to the output of thirty power plants. According to the American Council on an Energy Efficient Economy, the improved standards for appliances, including furnaces, water heaters, and ranges will save an estimated 1.3 billion barrels of oil equivalent, more than the 1 billion barrels estimated for all of the Atlantic.

Enhanced Recovery

Many of the nation's already developed onshore wells still contain oil, yet the companies have stopped production there because of low oil prices. Going back and pumping the remaining oil from these wells would contribute significantly to the nation's energy reserves and cost less than having to pay for the environmental costs associated with offshore drilling.

How You Can Save Energy

Energy efficiency begins at home. There are many things you can do to help reduce the nation's dependency on fossil fuels. By conserving energy, you'll not only help protect the nation's coast from offshore oil drilling and prevent global warming, but you'll lower your monthly utility and gasoline bills as well.

The tips outlined here are just a few of the many ways you can save energy. You can find more information from a variety of sources, including such environmental organizations as NRDC (see Appendix D for addresses) and the Rocky Mountain Institute (1739 Snowmass Creek Road, Snowmass, CO 81654). A very helpful guide to energy saving has been published by The EarthWorks Group (Box 25, Berkeley, CA 94709) in association with Pacific Gas & Electric. It is called *30 Simple Energy Things You Can Do to Save the Earth*. Many other utility companies also offer free advice on how to save energy. Contact yours.

- **Drive less.** Every day America's fleet of 135 million automobiles burns 82 million gallons of gas. By leaving just 1 percent of those cars idle one day a week, we could save 42 million gallons a year.

- **Buy a more fuel-efficient car.** Check the specs before you buy. There are several models that get way above the 26.5 mpg standard. Write for a free copy of Gas Mileage Guide, Consumer Information Center, Pueblo, CO 81009. It lists gas mileage for each make and model.

- **Keep your car tuned and tires properly inflated for better mileage.** A well-tuned car uses up to 9 percent less gasoline than a neglected car. Improperly inflated tires can waste up to 5 percent of a car's fuel.

Consider stripper wells, for example. Stripper wells are single wells that produce on average 2.7 barrels of oil a day. A survey conducted by the National Stripper Well Association shows that in 1987, nearly 452,000 stripper wells produced 4.46 million barrels of oil. But since 1980, an enormous number of stripper wells have been abandoned due to low oil prices. In 1980, 6,614 wells were officially abandoned. In 1986—the year the bottom fell out of the oil market—the number jumped to 19,233 wells. And that's just the number officially reported to state and federal authorities. According to the association, the total is much, much higher.

- **Carpool.** Americans drive 1 billion miles a day commuting to and from work. If each commuter car carried just one more person, we'd save 219 million gallons of gas a year.

- **Use mass transit.** A 50 percent increase in transit ridership over current levels could save more than 126 billion gallons of gas over the next twenty years.

- **Use energy-efficient appliances.** It takes the equivalent of nearly 185 million gallons of oil a day to run America's refrigerators, washers, dryers, and air conditioners. You can now buy appliances that use as little as one-third the energy.

- **Lower your thermostat and tune up your furnace.** If we all lowered our thermostats by 6 degrees Fahrenheit over a 24-hour period, we'd save 21 million gallons of oil every day. Tuning up your furnace can increase its efficiency by 5 percent.

- **Insulate your hot water heater and lower its thermostat.** Your hot water heater is your home's second largest energy user. You can save 6 percent of your water heating energy bill by lowering the temperature 10 degrees Fahrenheit. Insulating it will save even more.

- **Weatherize your house.** Nearly half the energy used to heat your home escapes through windows and doors. Caulking and weatherstripping cracks will save energy. Consider replacing windows with ones with double panes.

- **Use energy-efficient light bulbs.** High-efficiency fluorescent bulbs burn about one-fourth the kilowatt-hours as traditional bulbs. If America's 1 billion light sockets were equipped with high-efficiency bulbs, we could save 2.5 billion gallons of oil.

Stripper well executives estimate that 90,000 stripper wells were shut down in 1987 alone, taking out of production an estimated 300,000 barrels of oil per day, or 110 million barrels for the year.

According to the Department of Energy, 30 percent of the known crude oil in eight oil-producing states had been abandoned by 1980, and the figure grew to 40 percent in 1987. While much of the nation's known oil cannot be recovered because of geological or economic limitations, experts estimate that 100 billion barrels could become economical if prices are high enough to encourage technological advances.

Right now, according to the Department of Energy, more effective use of existing technologies like improved waterflooding and in-filling could recover an estimated additional 15 billion barrels of oil out of abandoned wells. That's nearly equal to the total identified U.S. energy resources in federal offshore waters.

Some success in the area of enhanced recovery has already been achieved. *The Wall Street Journal* writes about an Alberta, Canada, oil production company that inserted seven-inch diameter pipes as electrodes into several two-thousand-foot wells and passed a low-voltage electric current to electrodes buried elsewhere in the reservoir. The current flowed through the heavy oil reservoir, heating it. Production from each well jumped to seventy barrels a day from thirty barrels.

National Energy Policy Reform

The Interior Department's offshore leasing program is not the product of meaningful least-cost planning that analyzes alternatives to drilling in the nation's sensitive coastal areas. Least-cost planning evaluates new energy sources—both efficiency or conserved resources and supply resources—on a level economic playing field. The cost of different resources, including quantified environmental damage costs as well as internalized economic costs, are compared. Energy resources are chosen in the order of cost, from the lowest cost to the highest, until the entire need for energy services is satisfied.

Least-cost planning is already being practiced with success in various parts of the country. In the Pacific Northwest, for example, Congress mandated the creation of a governmental agency to plan for and acquire electricity in a least-cost fashion. The Northwest Power Planning Council found that a wide range of energy efficiency measures not currently being pursued had economic priority over the building of new power plants because they could provide the same amount of energy at lower environmental costs.

The California Energy Commission has operated under least-cost principles for over a dozen years under leadership from both political parties. The state has discovered and implemented a broad range of efficiency alternatives that are cheaper, faster, more flexible, and less environmentally disruptive than new energy supplies. As a result, California uses less than its share of oil and gas, and about one-third less

Photo by Chris Calwell

More solar plants like this one in California's Mojave Desert will help America end its dependence on fossil fuels.

energy per unit of economic output than the nation as a whole. State policy has developed efficiency resources that save much more oil and gas than could be found off the coast. Ratepayers saved billions of dollars, new conventional power plants didn't need to be built, and oil import reduction goals were met.

The results of California's program are dramatic: Over the next two decades, the state will have saved substantially more energy solely as a result of state policies than could be produced off its shores. According to the California Energy Commission, its program will have saved 61 million barrels of oil equivalent per year before the year 2000, rising to 78 million barrels by 2007.

The same result can be seen from aggregate oil and gas consumption statistics: In terms of oil and gas usage per unit of economic activity, the commission calculates that California already consumes less than the rest of the nation by some 150 million barrels of oil per year. In other words, California saves an amount of oil and gas that is equal to the estimated resource off the Northern and Southern California and Eastern Florida planning areas every twenty-one years. This achievement is all the more remarkable because it occurs almost entirely in the utility sector; the energy efficiency of automobiles, and, to a lesser extent, the level of investment in mass transit, is decided at the federal level.

Other tactics that could improve the nation's energy security are also being ignored by the federal government. One way would be to emphasize government action over market mechanisms. The government's decision to decontrol oil prices after years of price regulation achieved little to end the nation's dependency on foreign oil. That is because market forces seek to obtain energy supplies at the lowest cost. The market does not consider whether oil comes from Texas or the Persian Gulf; it simply considers price and availability. Because the market has been flooded with a glut of cheap oil from the Mideast in recent years, import levels remain high. Government action, on the other hand, could do much to lower import levels by reducing the demand for oil. The government could place taxes on oil to reduce consumption, establish import quotas, or take action to reduce the need for oil.

It is becoming clear to an increasing number of American voters that the nation's energy policy needs to be revised. Until that occurs, the country's security, economy, and environmental health remain at risk. The responsibility for making national energy policy ultimately rests with the president. He could do much to put the nation on the right track.

Specifically, the president should require development of a national least-cost energy plan to begin immediately. Such a plan would ensure that energy needs are met in the most cost-effective way and allow energy efficiency and renewable energy resources to compete with conventional resources on a level playing field.

The president should also increase federal support of research, development, and commercialization of energy efficiency and renewable energy sources. These have been neglected in recent years. The country requires new sources of energy that are not depletable and do not pollute. The boom-and-bust approach to renewable energy during the past decade must be replaced by a true national commitment to gradual and steady progress.

Biofuels, wind energy, geothermal energy, and solar power all have enormous potential to contribute to the country's energy future. Solar photovoltaics that produce electricity directly from sunlight deserve special emphasis, because they have the potential to supply power to homes and industries across the nation. Photovoltaic costs are now falling rapidly, but the once dominant U.S. industry is now being challenged by rivals in Europe and Japan that get more generous government support. If U.S. support of photovoltaics is not strengthened, not only will our use of this essential technology be slowed, but our leadership of a key strategic industry will also be jeopardized.

The president should also propose legislation that will increase the fuel economy of new automobiles and light trucks to 45 miles per gallon and 35 miles per gallon, respectively, by the year 2000. Attainment of these targets should be supported by an increased "gas guzzler" tax, a "gas sipper" rebate for efficient vehicles, and a gasoline tax to encourage increasing the efficiency of all vehicles.

Finally, the president should make the slowing of global warming a central goal of U.S. energy policy. Steps should be taken to establish national targets for overall efficiency and the reduction of carbon dioxide emissions. By emphasizing clean-burning energy over fossil fuels, the nation could significantly lower its production of greenhouse gases.

Ocean Sanctuary

While reform of the nation's energy policy will go a long way toward shifting the country away from its dependency on fossil fuels and to clean energy resources, more is necessary to achieve permanent protection of coastal resources. Citizen involvement in the lease sale process is an effective way to protect the coast on a site-by-site basis, but it is no substitute for a federal law that would permanently prohibit offshore oil drilling in sensitive areas. Such a law has already been proposed by a bipartisan coalition of congressional representatives from every Atlantic and Pacific coastal state.

The Ocean Protection Act of 1990 (H.R. 3751) would ban oil drilling on certain portions of the OCS, including 145 miles off of the entire California coast; 100 miles seaward from the shores of Oregon, Washington, and Alaska, as well as from Florida, Georgia, South Carolina, Virginia, Delaware, New Hampshire, and Maine; 125 miles off the coasts of New Jersey, New York, Connecticut, and Rhode Island; 175 miles off North Carolina; 50 miles off Maryland and Massachusetts; and within the Georges Bank fishing grounds, located in deeper water off the Massachusetts coast. The bill also calls for canceling leases and permits already in

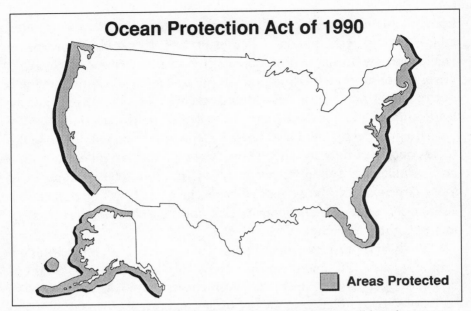

FIGURE 11 *The Ocean Protection Act of 1990 would place all but the western and central Gulf of Mexico off limits to new offshore oil drilling.*
Source: Central Coast Regional Studies Program

effect in southwestern Florida waters and in Bristol Bay, Alaska. In addition, it calls for a study on canceling lease sales in North Carolina. Not included in the bill's ban is most of the Gulf of Mexico, and specifically the coastal waters of Texas, Louisiana, Mississippi, and Alabama.

While the act would protect much of the OCS, it would still leave 93 percent of the nation's undiscovered, economically recoverable oil and gas, and 74 percent of the undiscovered oil and gas in the OCS available for production. The 5.5 billion barrels of oil and gas the act would put off limits amount to less than 40 percent of the cumulative savings the nation could realize by the year 2020 if the Corporate Automobile Fuel Economy Standards were raised to 40 mpg for cars and 30 mpg for light trucks by the year 2000.

Public support of this bill, or one like it, is crucial for passage. By making your opinion known, you can help convince Congress of the act's importance. Permanent protection is a realistic goal: Congress has already showed its willingness to protect the nation's resources from the environmental consequences of the oil industry in the wake of the *Exxon Valdez* disaster by passing oil spill liability legislation.

The Comprehensive Oil Pollution Liability and Compensation Bill (H.R. 1465) and its Senate counterpart (S. 686) would raise existing federal liability limits on tankers, barges, offshore platforms, deep-water ports, and other oil facilities. Cleanup and compensation costs beyond those paid by spillers would come out of a fund created by taxing domestic and imported oil. The bill would also set various standards and requirements to try to prevent spills. And, importantly, the bill would allow states to have tougher laws. Twenty-eight states have their own oil spill liability statutes. Nineteen set no limits on the amount that should be spent by oil companies or carriers on cleanup costs.

The oil spill liability law will assure quick action and guarantee that polluters pay. The Ocean Protection Act of 1990 will provide additional insurance. By putting portions of the nation's coastal waters permanently off limits to oil drilling, a major source of oil spills—not to mention air and water pollution and onshore industrialization—will be eliminated. The old chestnut "an ounce of prevention is worth a pound of cure" has never rung truer.

Appendix A

THE LEASE SALE PROCESS

The OCS leasing process is divided into two phases: pre-lease and post-lease sale. The pre-lease stage is what precedes the actual sale of offshore tracts by the federal government to the oil industry. It is managed by the Minerals Management Service (MMS), a branch of the DOI.

Pre-Lease Sale

1. Call for Information and Nominations and Notice of Intent to Prepare Environmental Impact Statement. The Call for Information, published in the *Federal Register*, is the first step in the pre-lease sale process. It accomplishes two things. First, it invites potential bidders to nominate areas and indicate levels of interest in OCS leasing. Second, it allows state and local governments and members of the public to comment on these areas or any other topics of concern about offshore drilling, including negative nominations requesting that potential areas be deleted from the lease sale.

Both the Call and the Notice of Intent, which is also published in the *Federal Register*, are sent to the governor of each affected state for comments. The governor is asked to identify issues and areas of concern that should be considered in the development of the initial leasing proposal. The Call for Information and Notice of Intent are the first opportunity for anybody to comment on a proposed sale.

The Call for Information also solicits comments from agencies and interested parties on any environmental effects and conflicts, as well as coastal zone consistency concerns. States, local governments, and the public have the opportunity to comment on areas or topics of concern. Comments from all parties are due forty-five days after the Call is published. A local government can also present concerns on potential environmental impacts and conflicts to the MMS. The MMS must respond to the governor's comments; thus, to maximize effectiveness, local governments and the public should forward their comments to the governor and request that they be incorporated into the state's comments. The public can also help influence their local government officials' comments.

2. Area Identification.   About four months after the Call is published, the MMS completes its analysis of nominations and comments. (The exact time can vary considerably, as the timing is under control of the MMS. Times stated here are approximations only.) The director of the MMS then specifies areas where leasing is expected to occur based on comments received, identifying blocks either for further study or for possible deletion.

Following the announcement of Area Identification, the MMS sends the governor a response to the state's comments. The MMS advises the governor on how comments were employed in the Area Identification process and how they will be used in the development of alternatives and mitigation measures to be analyzed in the Environmental Impact Statement (EIS). Because the MMS has no statutory responsibility to respond to local governments or citizens, it is important to have all local and public concerns incorporated into the governor's comments.

3. Scoping/Draft Environmental Impact Statement.   Prior to initiating the EIS, scoping meetings may be held by the MMS to define issues and receive comments relating to the proposed lease sale EIS. State and local governments and the public have the opportunity to provide input at this stage, either at the hearings or by written comments. Anyone can provide comments to the MMS on areas of concern, proposed alternatives, proposed mitigation measures, and any other local issues of importance that should be analyzed in the EIS. Unfortunately, because a lease sale EIS covers such a large area, specific concerns often do not get addressed. However, if anyone wishes to ultimately challenge the MMS document for not addressing such issues, it would be critical to be able to show that they were identified early in the process.

About one year after the Call is published, a Draft EIS (DEIS) is prepared by the MMS. It describes the planning area, identifies potential environmental, socioeconomic, and cumulative effects of proposed oil and gas activities, and discusses potential mitigation measures to reduce these impacts. The document also analyzes alternatives to the proposed action. The availability of the Draft EIS is announced in the *Federal Register* in a Notice of Availability.

4. Comments/Hearings. A sixty-day comment period follows the release of the DEIS to the public. During this time, public hearings are held in the affected region to provide a forum for public comment. Comments received from the public hearings or in writing are considered in the preparation of the Final EIS. Anyone can submit comments to the MMS on the adequacy of the document. Comments should focus on potential local impacts that were not identified or were misidentified and should include suggestions for mitigation measures. Unfortunately, the MMS must simply respond to comments, not necessarily incorporate them into the final document. However, it is still important to comment, especially if a challenge to the document's adequacy is being contemplated.

5. Final EIS/Secretarial Issue Document. Three to five months (again, the exact time is controlled by the MMS) after the public hearings, a Final EIS incorporating all comments is released. Next, a Secretarial Issue Document (SID) is prepared to summarize the conclusions of the EIS and consider other issues, such as state recommendations.

6. Proposed Notice of Sale. The Proposed Notice of Sale is issued about one month after the Final EIS is filed. This Notice provides information on which blocks are available for leasing, the stipulations for given blocks, the bidding system, and the length of the primary lease term.

7. Governor's Comments. The Proposed Notice is sent to the governor, requesting comments on size, timing, or location of the sale. The governor has sixty days in which to consult with local government leaders to hear their concerns and then formulate a reply. Pursuant to Section 19 of the Outer Continental Shelf Lands Act, the governor may advise the Secretary of the Interior to delete certain tracts and recommend stipulations to be included in the final lease sale. The secretary must then respond to the governor's recommendation or implement any alternative identified in consultation with the governor to provide a reasonable balance between the national interest and the well-being of the citizens of the affected state. The secretary can reject a governor's recommendations on the basis of the national interest, and the secretary's decision to reject recommendations may be overturned on judicial review only if found to be "arbitrary and capricious."

8. Final Notice of Sale. After comments are received, the secretary prepares a final decision memorandum analyzing all issues and updating any information that may differ from data given in the earlier Proposed Notice of Sale. If the secretary decides to proceed with the sale, a final Notice of Sale must be issued and must appear in the *Federal Register* no less than thirty days before the sale is to be conducted. It specifies the blocks to be offered, the date of the lease sale, and other pertinent information.

9. Sale. Not less than thirty days after the final notice is published, a sale is conducted by the appropriate MMS regional office. Qualified bidders are invited to submit sealed bids, which are opened and read at the public sale.

10. Decision to Accept or Reject Bids. Bids are accepted or rejected on lease blocks containing potentially viable prospects. The secretary has up to ninety days after the receipt of a bid to accept or reject it. Normally, bids are accepted and leases issued within a one- to two-month period.

11. Issuance of Lease. Once awarded, a lease grants the right to explore, develop, and produce oil and gas for a specific term on a specific tract (usually 5,760 acres). The lessee has five to ten years to begin exploratory drilling, depending on the individual lease term. The lease is extended for as long as oil and gas are commercially produced. Lease rentals and royalties are paid to the federal government. A 1986 amendment to OCSLA enabled affected coastal states to receive a share of these federal royalties.

Post-Lease Sale

After the sale is completed, there are fifteen post-lease steps.

1. Plan of Exploration. Oil companies must prepare a Plan of Exploration (POE) describing the proposed drilling site or sites and the planned exploratory operations to be used in determining whether or not commercially recoverable oil and gas reserves are present on the block. This plan includes a detailed description of all necessary activities and equipment, the location of each proposed well, and the structure and formations expected to be drilled, as well as a complete activities timetable.

Before activities begin, the lessee must submit an environmental report as well as plans for oil spill contingencies and critical operations and curtailment activities.

2. Environmental Analysis. Copies of the complete POE are distributed to affected states, federal agencies, and the public for review. Local governments and citizens have the opportunity to comment to the MMS on the plan. However, the MMS is under no obligation to consider the comments they receive. The MMS forwards the POE to the Environmental Protection Agency (EPA) and the U.S. Department of Army Corps of Engineers (COE). Meanwhile, the MMS has thirty days to perform a technical analysis and an environmental review to determine whether or not the proposed project will require a formal Environmental Impact Statement (EIS).

3. Approval or Disapproval. Within thirty days after the Exploration Plan has been deemed complete, the MMS must approve, require modification of, or disapprove the plan. Approval generally hinges on whether or not the plan conforms to the provisions of the lease, the OCSLA, and other pertinent regulations.

4. Consistency Certification. The Coastal Zone Management Act, administered by the Department of Commerce through the National Oceanic and Atmospheric Administration's Office of Ocean Coastal and Resource Management, requires that applicants for exploration or development and production plans for activities affecting land and water uses in the coastal zone must certify to the state that the proposed activities will be consistent with the state's approved program. The state has three months in which to concur or object to proposed activities. If a decision cannot be reached within three months, an extension can be granted. However, if no decision is reached at the end of six months, approval is assumed.

The consistency process provides local governments and citizens with the opportunity to comment on exploration and development and production activities.

5. National Pollutant Discharge Elimination System (NPDES)/Department of Army Section Permits. Under the NPDES, a lessee is required to apply to the EPA for discharge authorization at least 180 days before discharge is to begin. Before making a decision, the EPA invites comments from states and other interested parties.

6. Application for Permit to Drill (APD). Once an Exploration Plan is approved and all affected states concur with the lessee's consistency certification, a lessee must submit and receive approval of an APD before beginning exploratory drilling operations. The APD essentially implements the POE.

7. Exploratory Drilling. Once all permits are obtained, the lessee can begin drilling. Information generated by the exploratory drilling is collected and analyzed to decide whether further drilling is warranted.

8. Development and Production Plan (DPP). After completing the drilling necessary to delineate the discovered productive area, the lessee must submit and receive approval of a DPP before beginning production. This plan is similar to an Exploration Plan and is subjected to an analogous review process (see Post-Lease Sale, section 1). The plan describes all the work necessary to achieve sustained production; all drilling vessels, platforms, pipelines, or other facilities and operations that will be involved; surface and bottom-hole locations of each proposed well; interpretations of all relevant geological and geophysical data; environmental safeguards to be implemented; safety standards and features; the expected rate of development and production; and other relevant information the MMS may require. In addition, an oil spill contingency plan, environmental report, and certification of consistency are also required.

9. Consistency Certification. The plan, environmental report, and consistency certification must be submitted to the state's coastal zone management agency for review. It has two months to determine whether the activities described in the plan are consistent with its program.

10. Environmental Assessment (EA). The Development and Production Plan undergoes an environmental review similar to the one conducted for an Exploration Plan. An EA is prepared to evaluate the likely impacts and to determine if the proposed project has a significant enough effect on the environment. An EIS is generally prepared.

11. Scoping Hearing/Environmental Impact Statement. The issues to be analyzed in the EIS are determined as a result of scoping hearings. Cooperative agreements may be formed by the Department of the Interior and affected states to generate a combination Environmental Impact Statement/Environmental Impact Report (EIS/R), in order to facilitate efficient review and approval of development and production plans.

12. Coordination and Consultation with Affected States and Local Governments. The OCS Lands Act provides for the governor of any affected state and the executive of any affected local government to be given the opportunity to make recommendations regarding the DPP. Recommendations offered during this consultation process are accepted if they are deemed to provide for a reasonable balance between the national interest and the well-being of the citizens of the affected states. However, as previously mentioned, the state's actual influence is limited, because the Secretary of the Interior is not obligated to accept these recommendations.

13. State/Local Permitting Process. Projects that cross state waters or require offshore facilities in state waters, such as subsea pipelines and marine terminals, may require specific state permits.

In addition, after the DPP is submitted, an applicant will also initiate the local permitting process for onshore facilities such as processing plants, pipelines, supply bases, and marine terminals. These onshore components require separate development plan applications and undergo extensive review from the county planning departments and air pollution control districts. The local environmental review process usually results in a joint report that analyzes both onshore and offshore components of the project. The onshore permitting process can take several years and requires substantial input from county staff.

14. Application for Permit to Drill (APD). An APD is filed with the district MMS/OCS office by the lessee or operator. A lessee may not drill any well until approval of an APD has been received.

15. Development Wells Drilled/Production Commences. After the APD is approved, all other permits granted, and the necessary offshore and onshore facilities built, development wells are drilled and production begins.

Appendix B

OFFSHORE OIL AND GAS DEVELOPMENT REGULATIONS

Numerous federal, state, and local regulations and agencies influence offshore oil and gas development. Management of offshore resources is divided among federal, state, and local jurisdictions and is also split among several different federal, state, and local agencies, each with its own management responsibilities. In the case of offshore oil and gas resources, the federal government controls development in the ocean area extending from three to 200-300 miles offshore, the state government generally controls the ocean belt from the shoreline to three miles offshore, and local governments have permitting authority over development facilities located onshore and over air quality onshore and in the ocean area out to three miles.

The coastal zone is defined as land and water extending seaward to the state's outer limit of jurisdiction (generally three miles from the mean high tide line), including offshore islands, and extending inland generally one thousand yards from the mean high tide line. In significant coastal estuarine habitats and recreational areas it extends inland to the first major ridgeline paralleling the sea or five miles from the mean high tide line of the sea, whichever is less. In developed urban areas the zone generally extends inland less than a thousand yards.

Federal Regulations and Agencies

At the federal level, the major law regulating offshore oil development is the Outer Continental Shelf Lands Act Amendments (OCSLAA) of 1978, which amended the 1953 Outer Continental Shelf Lands Act (OCSLA). The major federal agency involved is the Department of the Interior's Minerals Management Service (MMS), whose primary function is to implement the OCSLAA and to manage the extensive government royalties derived from offshore oil development. Some thirty other federal laws also affect offshore oil and gas development in one way or another.

The Outer Continental Shelf Lands Act and Its Amendments. The OCS Lands Act of August 7, 1953, authorized the Secretary of the Interior to grant mineral leases and to prescribe regulations governing oil and gas activities on OCS lands. The OCSLA defines the OCS as ". . . all submerged lands lying seaward and outside of the area of lands beneath navigable waters as defined in Section 2 of the Submerged Lands Act and of which the subsoil and seabed appertain to the United States and are subject to its jurisdiction and control." The OCSLA established the importance of developing the mineral resources of the continental shelf in an expeditious and orderly manner. The act also recognized the need for safely conducting oil and gas operations and using technology and procedures intended to minimize the likelihood of blowouts, fires, spills, and interference with other uses of the offshore waters.

The act was amended on September 18, 1978. The purposes of the amendments were:

- to establish policies and procedures that expedite exploration and development on the OCS in order to achieve national economic and energy goals, assure national security, reduce dependence on foreign sources, and maintain a favorable balance of payments in world trade;
- to balance orderly energy resource development with protection of the human, marine, and coastal environments;
- to ensure the public a fair and equitable return on the resources of the OCS;
- to encourage development of new and improved technology in order to eliminate or minimize the risk of damage to the human, marine, and coastal environments;
- to assure that affected states, through state and local governments, have timely access to information regarding OCS activities and opportunities to review, comment, and participate in policy and planning decisions;
- to establish an oil spill liability fund; and
- to establish a fishermen's contingency fund.

The OCSLA was amended again in 1986 by the Outer Continental Shelf Lands Act Amendments of 1985.

National Environmental Policy Act. The NEPA sets out policies and goals for protection of the environment and requires the preparation of an

Environmental Impact Statement (EIS) prior to major federal actions that could have a significant impact on the environment. Upon receipt of either a Plan of Exploration (POE) or a Development and Production Plan (DPP), the MMS conducts an environmental assessment that provides a brief analysis for determining whether or not an EIS should be prepared.

Coastal Zone Management Act. The CZMA is administered by the Department of Commerce through the National Oceanic and Atmospheric Administration's Office of Ocean Coastal and Resource Management. The act provides for state review of POEs and DPPs that affect the land and water uses of the coastal zone. The CZMA also requires consistency of relevant activities in those plans with approved state coastal management programs.

Federal Water Pollution Control Act. Commonly known as the Clean Water Act, it establishes standards and a permit program for "point source" discharges of pollutants; establishes liability for oil spills and provides for federal cleanup efforts through a national contingency plan; and requires the U.S. Army Corps of Engineers (COE) to issue permits for discharges of dredged fill material into navigable waters or wetlands. In-water discharges of pollutants generated by OCS operations must comply with the limitations and restrictions that are included in the applicable National Pollutant Discharge Elimination System (NPDES) permit.

Army Corps of Engineers Section 404/Section 10 Permit. The COE has the responsibility to protect and develop the nation's water resources and to regulate construction in waters of the United States. It regulates discharge of dredged or fill materials, construction in navigable waters, and transport of dredged material for dumping into ocean waters. Construction of a platform, pipeline, or offshore treatment and storage (OS&T) facility in navigable waters requires a Section 404/Section 10 permit.

Endangered Species Act. The ESA provides protection for listed plants and animals in both federal and state jurisdictions. It also requires that federal agencies consult with the U.S. Fish and Wildlife Service (FWS) and the National Marine Fisheries Service (NMFS) to ensure that any action authorized, funded, or carried out by the agency is not likely to jeopardize the continued existence of endangered or threatened species or result in the destruction of critical habitats. This is known as a Section 7 Consultation. Where such species are present, either the FWS or the NMFS must evaluate potential impacts from OCS operations.

Other Federal Regulations. The Clean Air Act sets general guidelines and minimum air quality standards on a nationwide basis in order to protect and enhance the quality of the nation's air resources. The Marine Mammal Protection Act prohibits harassment, hunting, capturing, or killing of marine mammals without a permit from either the Secretary of the Interior or the Secretary of Commerce, depending upon the species of marine mammal involved. The Ports and Waterways Safety Act covers navigational safety. The National Historic Preservation Act provides for the protection of historic and prehistoric archaeological resources.

State Regulations

Although states do not have direct authority to regulate oil and gas development on the OCS, the federal OCSLAA does grant those states that have enacted federally approved coastal management programs the right to review and determine whether federal proposals comply with state plans. Twenty-nine of the nation's thirty-five coastal states and territories have federally approved coastal programs, including all of the Pacific and Atlantic coastal states, with the exception of Georgia.

California's program is a good example. The California Coastal Act of 1976 established the foundation of the California Coastal Zone Management Program. It is administered by a governmental agency, the California Coastal Commission (CCC). The CCC has permit authority over project components in state waters and retains appeal authority over certain development and geographic areas in the onshore portion of the coastal zone. In addition, the CCC performs federal consistency review for all projects involving federal actions, including proposed development in federal waters or on federal lands that may have direct effects on the coastal zone. Any development within the coastal zone requires a Coastal Development Permit (CDP). Counties and cities with approved Local Coastal Plans have permit jurisdiction within the coastal zone. Therefore, facilities like a marine terminal require two CDPs, one from the CCC and one from the county.

Appendix C

MODEL LETTERS AND PRESS ANNOUNCEMENTS

Writing letters to elected officials and the media is an effective way of calling attention to the issue of offshore oil drilling. By expressing your concerns to decisionmakers, you can help shape public policy. Ask your local government representatives to enact resolutions opposing offshore oil drilling. At the state and federal level, ask your elected officials to vote for permanent protection.

Letters to the editor and opinion pieces written for newspapers also keep the issue in the public eye. When voicing your opinion, make your concerns heartfelt. You can also attract media attention by staging press conferences, public debates, and demonstrations. To alert the media, you need to distribute press advisories, followed by press releases. Once you get their attention, you need to simplify the message in fact sheet format.

Here are a few examples of model letters, editorials, local government resolutions, press announcements, and fact sheets.

MODEL LETTER TO ELECTED OFFICIAL

Representative George Miller
367 Civic Drive, Suite 14
Pleasant Hill, CA 94523

Dear Representative:
   I was appalled to learn that the "Central" California
Coast was not included in the moratorium on offshore oil
drilling. This area, known to the Senate as "lease sale #119,"
covers 1.7 million acres of water stretching from Sonoma to
Monterey. As responsible citizens, we cannot allow offshore
drilling for the following reasons:
   Were the Coast and Bay Area to be ravaged by an oil spill
either from transportation tankers, processing tankers, or the
drilling platforms themselves, the environmental destruction
would be devastating. The ten-million-gallon spill from the
Exxon Valdez covered 2,600 square miles—exactly comparable to
the coastline from Point Arena to Point Sur, including the San
Francisco Bay. A report by the CCRSP (Central Coast Regional
Studies Program, created by the counties bordering the proposed development) estimated that four spills, including one
of at least 15 million gallons, would be likely over the life
of the project. As responsible citizens we cannot allow this
to happen.
   Ironically, in spite of all the risk involved, we would
actually gain very little oil. The CCRSP estimates that the
amount of recoverable oil would be between 549 and 775 million
barrels. At current national consumption rates, this amount
would last only one to one and a half months. Even the most
minor of conservative efforts, such as improved automobile and
residential efficiency standards, could make this up more than
ten times over.
   As your constituent, I will be watching whether or not you
vigorously protect California's entire coastline from offshore
oil drilling. No offshore drilling should be permitted on the
West Coast: the economic gain is minuscule and temporary at
best.

   Sincerely,

MODEL LETTERS TO THE EDITOR

Cost of Drilling?

Editor—A postscript to John Kara's letter (Chronicle, March 5) regarding President Bush's likely approval of oil drilling off the California coast; he stated that the oil pumped from offshore would last maybe 10 to 15 years.

In fact, the estimate of the amount of oil off the coast of Mendocino is 30 days' worth. One month on the road in exchange for the Mendocino coast. I'd rather walk.

RACHEL HEYMAN
San Francisco

Ocean Sanctuary

Editor—President Bush is about to make an historic announcement about offshore oil drilling. What we don't need is another Band-Aid solution of delays that will eventually run out, leaving our oceans vulnerable again in a few months or years. What we do need is permanent protection: ocean sanctuary.

Awareness of the threats and damage done to the ocean and coastal environments has reached unparalleled heights; the disastrous oil spill in Alaska has angered and horrified most of the nation. It is clear that further pollution and degradation of the ocean must stop.

Ocean sanctuary legislation would provide permanent protection for all coastal areas, while encouraging energy conservation and the development of clean, renewable energy resources. It encompasses concerns about oil development, hazardous and toxic wastes, and dumping and incineration. It also enhances fisheries.

Representative Barbara Boxer, D-San Francisco/Marin, has introduced HR 3751. This is the National Ocean Protection Act, which would permanently ban offshore oil drilling along the Atlantic and Pacific coasts and Alaska. This bill is an important first step toward creating a National Ocean Sanctuary, which would permanently protect our oceans from additional threats of toxic and nuclear waste dumping, incineration, and deep-sea strip mining.

We urge citizens to write their representatives and ask them to support the ocean protection legislation, HR 3751. The government is bound to respond to the will of the people. So spread the word among your schools, service organizations, recreational clubs, church groups, professional organizations, neighbors, and friends. If we want to leave a breathable, livable world for our children and grandchildren, we must save our oceans and our atmosphere now.

DONNA NIETO
TERESA KAPLAN
Ocean Sanctuary
Coordinating Committee
Mendocino

MODEL EDITORIAL

Why We Don't Want Offshore Drilling

Many think a ban is necessary to protect the fragile Florida coast

By Lisa Speer
and Ann Whitfield

President Bush will soon decide the fate of offshore oil development plans off the Florida Keys and the Everglades. After years of controversy and temporary delays, it is time to put this issue to rest permanently by protecting South Florida from oil drilling.

Campaigning in Florida during the 1988 election, Bush promised to reevaluate plans for offshore drilling along South Florida's rich and fragile coast.

To fulfill that promise, he appointed a federal task force, which recently submitted a secret report to the president outlining various options he could pursue with respect to drilling off South Florida. The president's decision on how to proceed with the drilling issue is imminent.

Concern over the impact of oil spills and other pollution generated in massive quantities by the offshore oil industry has led environmentalists, along with the entire Florida congressional delegation and Gov. Bob Martinez, to call for permanent protection from oil development for waters off South Florida. But so far their calls have been ignored by the Bush administration.

For example, none of the options identified by the task force, which is headed by the pro-oil Secretary of the Interior, Manuel Lujan, reportedly include permanent protection for South Florida.

Instead, the options are said to include only token delays for further leasing. And two of the three options don't address the most imminent threat to this region—drilling near the Keys that could begin, under existing leases, later this year.

From Key West to Miami to Apalachicola, Floridians of all political stripes have made it clear that they will not tolerate the threat of oil to the very resources that are the basis of the state's tourist economy—clean water, beautiful beaches, unspoiled coral reefs.

The Exxon Valdez disaster demonstrated the oil industry's ability to destroy in minutes ecosystems that nature took centuries to create.

The threat to South Florida is all too clear. Testimony provided to the task force by Everglades National Park officials and others chronicled the dangers of spills and massive water pollution generated by the offshore oil industry. The small amount of oil projected by the federal government to underlie the region—a mere thirty-four days' worth at current U.S. consumption rates—could easily be replaced by readily available energy conservation measures. The environmental price of oil development in the area clearly outweighs the transient benefits of extracting a month's worth of oil.

In a report commissioned by the task force, the National Academy of Sciences concluded that ecological information is "inadequate and unreliable" to support any decisionmaking on drilling off South Florida. However, the academy concluded that knowledge about the physical oceanography of the area is sufficient to predict that oil spills off the coast would likely wash ashore on Florida's beaches.

No further study or delays will change the oceanography of South Florida or the fact that spilled oil will quickly wind up on Florida's beaches.

Further information and more delays will not alter the inescapable conclusion that offshore oil development poses unacceptable risks to the unique and nationally significant natural resources of the Keys and the Everglades.

We can replace the oil thought to underlie this region with modest conservation measures; we can never replace the resources of the Keys and Everglades that oil may irrevocably destroy. For these reasons, it is time to permanently protect South Florida from offshore oil.

The president now has the opportunity to demonstrate his stated commitment to protecting the environment by supporting the bipartisan drive for permanent protection.

After years of controversy and conflict over offshore drilling in South Florida, the public is in no mood for hollow symbolic gestures or short-term delays. It is time to get serious about protecting the Keys and the Everglades, not for future desecration but for future generations.

Lisa Speer is a senior staff scientist with the Natural Resources Defense Council, a national environmental organization. Ann Whitfield is executive director of the Florida Public Interest Research Group.

MODEL GOVERNMENT RESOLUTION

Local government often uses resolutions to help guide policy decisions. Citizens can encourage local governing bodies to adopt appropriate resolutions concerning coastal protection.

A Resolution of the Board of Control of the Central Coast OCS Regional Studies Program in Response to the Minerals Management Service
Call for Information and Nominations for Lease Sale Number 119

WHEREAS, the Department of the Interior proposes to lease 1.7 million acres of coastal waters off the six central California counties of Sonoma, Marin, San Francisco, San Mateo, Santa Cruz, and Monterey, and

WHEREAS, the Department of the Interior has asked for public comments in response to their Call for Information for Lease Sale Number 119 published on November 16, 1988, in the Federal Register, and

WHEREAS, the central California coast is one of the most pristine and magnificent coastlines in the world, and

WHEREAS, the central coast environment supports a crucial economic resource to Californians including: a renewable commercial and sport fishing industry and an annual multimillion-dollar tourist and recreation industry, and

WHEREAS, the central coast waters provide a habitat for abundant and diverse species of marine mammals, fish, and birds, including several endangered species, and

WHEREAS, the central coast contains three designated national marine sanctuaries, many areas of special biological significance, and numerous important marine research facilities, and

WHEREAS, proposed oil and gas exploration and development activities threaten fishing, due to seismic activities, displacement of fishing grounds, competition for limited harbor facilities, and disposal of toxic wastes into prime fishing grounds, and

WHEREAS, oil platforms, offshore storage and treatment facilities, marine terminals, and onshore processing facilities would profoundly diminish the rural, scenic quality of the coastline and could lead to a serious decline in tourism and recreation activities, and

WHEREAS, prevailing winds would blow offshore drilling emissions onshore, thereby interfering with the ability of coastal communities to achieve and maintain state and federal air quality attainment standards, and

WHEREAS, many key sites of interest for oil and gas development are adjacent to critical marine wildlife habitats, including the Gulf of the Farallones, Cordell Bank, and the A:o Nuevo State Reserve, and

WHEREAS, the Department of the Interior estimates a high probability for a large oil spill and acknowledges that only 5 to 15 percent of any oil spill can be cleaned up, and

WHEREAS, the oil available in Lease Sale Number 119 is estimated to contain only five to seven weeks of our nation's oil consumption needs, and

WHEREAS, current federal energy policies fail to adequately address alternative energy and energy efficiency programs such as improved auto fuel efficiency standards, and

WHEREAS, oil and gas exploration off the central California coast is a high-risk, short-term solution that ignores long-term environmental issues such as global warming, and

WHEREAS, oil and gas exploration and drilling operations off the central California coast will jeopardize unique and valuable coastal resources, and

WHEREAS, the proposed sale and resulting oil and gas exploration and drilling operations will result in conflicts with California coastal zone management policies and approved local coastal management plans, and

WHEREAS, leasing, exploration, development, and transportation activities resulting from Lease Sale Number 119 conflict with the policies of the OCS Lands Act as amended, the Clean Air Act, the Marine Mammals Act and the Endangered Species Act;

NOW THEREFORE BE IT RESOLVED, that for the reasons stated above, all tracts located in the Lease Sale Number 119 Call for Information should be defined as significant environmentally sensitive tracts, and

THEREFORE BE IT FURTHER RESOLVED, that the Board of Control of the Central Coast Regional Studies Program hereby offers negative nominations for all tracts proposed for inclusion in Lease Sale Number 119, and

BE IT FURTHER RESOLVED, that copies of this resolution and the attached technical comments in response to the Lease Sale Number 119 Call for Information be forwarded to Governor George Deukmejian, to the Regional Supervisor, Office of Leasing and Environment, MMS, Pacific OCS Region, as well as to the Chief, Offshore Leasing Management Division, MMS, Department of the Interior, Washington, D.C.

MODEL PRESS ADVISORY

For Immediate Release   Contact:Dorrie Smith
                                              Greenpeace
                                              (202) 462-1177

PUBLIC HEARINGS CAN STOP MOBIL

   On November 1, 1989, the Minerals Management Service
(MMS), the agency within the U.S. Department of the Interior
responsible for leasing and developing offshore oil and gas
resources published an environmental report on Mobil's proposed plan for oil and gas development forty miles off Cape
Hatteras. This famed report, negotiated by the MMS, Mobil,
and Governor Martin last summer, is a treatise on offshore
drilling as seen through the eyes of the federal government,
an avid proponent of offshore drilling. Public hearings on
the environmental report are scheduled for December 4-7 in
Manteo, Beaufort, Washington, and Raleigh, respectively.
   These hearings are a golden opportunity to tell the federal government whether or not you favor an invasion of
coastal North Carolina by multinational oil companies. Never
mind that the MMS is requiring advance registration by citizens who wish to speak and submit written testimony at the
hearing. These restrictions may simply mean that the MMS and
Mobil are worried about public opinion. Everyone is welcome
to come and speak. Perhaps, if the turnout is great enough,
the MMS will be forced to put aside these stifling restrictions and let the public speak.
       The public hearings will take place as follows:
       Monday—Manteo Public High School
       Tuesday—Duke Marine Lab Auditorium, Pivers Island
       Wednesday—Beaufort County Community College, Washington,
       N.C.
       Thursday—Velvet Cloak Inn, 1505 Hillsborough St., Raleigh

       All hearings are from 2:00 to 5:00pm and 7:00 to 10pm.

   Concerned citizens rallies will be held at 6:30pm prior to
the Beaufort and Raleigh hearings. All are welcome.

MODEL PRESS RELEASE

Coastal Protection Group
100 Ocean Street
Anytown, USA
Telephone: (415) 555-5555

Press Advisory: June 30, 1991   For more information:
FOR IMMEDIATE RELEASE   Jane Beach (415) 555-5555

COASTAL GROUP CALLS FOR AN END TO OFFSHORE OIL LEASING

(Anytown, USA) (June 30, 1991)—In a colorful public hearing that attracted more than one thousand local residents,
members of the Coastal Protection Group called upon officials
of the federal Minerals Management Service to remove the
coast off Anytown from consideration for offshore oil leasing.

Members of the Coastal Protection Group presented their
testimony at an official public hearing that gave residents
and local government officials the opportunity to participate
in the lease sale decision-making process.

"The environmental dangers associated with offshore oil
drilling are irrefutable," said Bob Surf, president of the
community group. "Oil drilling will jeopardize our coastal
way of life. An oil spill could wipe out our commercial
fishing industry as well our tourism-based economy. The
government is willing to risk all that for what amounts to be
less than twelve days of oil. The fact is, much more oil
than that could be obtained by enacting some energy efficiency measures."

The Coastal Protection Group is a nonprofit coalition of
citizen organizations fighting for the permanent ban of offshore oil drilling along the Anytown coast.

SAMPLE FACT SHEET

H.R. 3751
National Ocean Protection Act of 1990

The Ocean Protection Act is a simple bill to prohibit further offshore oil development off much of the United States coast. The specific language reads:

The Secretary [of the Interior] shall not issue a lease, permit, or license for the exploration for or extraction of oil and gas on or from submerged lands described in subsection (b) [listed below].

It does not prohibit offshore oil development in areas which have already been leased, with the exception of those southwest of Florida and in Bristol Bay listed below.

Areas Protected

Alaska:	100 miles	New Hampshire:	100 miles
California:	145 miles	New Jersey:	125 miles
Connecticut:	125 miles	New York:	125 miles
Delaware:	100 miles	North Carolina:	175 miles
Florida:	100 miles and all lands south of 26 degrees north latitude and east of 86 degrees west longitude	Oregon:	100 miles
		Rhode Island:	125 miles
		South Carolina:	100 miles
		Virginia:	100 miles
Georgia:	100 miles	Washington:	100 miles
Maine:	100 miles		
Maryland:	50 miles		
Massachusetts:	50 miles and waters shallower than 400 meters on the Georges Bank fishing grounds		

Lease "Buy-Backs"

The National Ocean Protection Act will cancel any lease or permit for offshore oil drilling with compensation to the permit holder for the following areas:

Any lands south of 26 degrees north latitude and east of 86 degrees west longitude (southwest Florida).

Any lands within the North Aleutian Basin (Bristol Bay).

The bill also requires the Department of Interior to study alternative methods of compensation for buying back leases off North Carolina.

Areas Not Protected

The only areas not protected from offshore oil drilling are the waters off the states of Texas, Louisiana, Mississippi, and Alabama.

Appendix D

RESOURCES

The Minerals Management Service of the Department of the Interior administers the offshore oil lease sale program. Write or call to be put on the MMS mailing list and to be notified of the exact dates for specific public participation opportunities.

U.S. Department of the Interior
Minerals Management Service (MMS)
1849 C Street, N.W.
Washington, DC 20240
(202) 208-3983

MMS Alaska Region
949 East 36th Avenue
Anchorage, AK 99508
(907) 261-4070

MMS Pacific Region
770 Paseo
Camarillo, CA 93010
(213) 894-3389

MMS Atlantic Region
381 Elden Street
Herndon, VA 22070
(703) 787-1113

MMS Gulf of Mexico Region
1201 Elmwood Park Boulevard
New Orleans, LA 70123-2394
(504) 736-2595

There are many groups that can provide information on offshore oil drilling and the lease sale process. These include the following, listed by state:

ALASKA

Greenpeace
Box 104432
Anchorage, AK 99510
(907) 277-8334

Northern Alaska Environmental Center
218 Driveway
Fairbanks, AK 99701
(907) 452-5021

Trustees for Alaska
725 Christenson Drive, Number 4
Anchorage, AK 99501
(907) 276-4244

ALABAMA
Mobile Bay Audubon Society
Box 9903
Mobile, AL 36609
(205) 666-2476

CALIFORNIA
American Oceans Campaign
2219 Main Street, Number 2B
Santa Monica, CA 90405
(213) 452-2206

Central Coast Regional Studies
   Program
116 New Montgomery Street
Suite 910
San Francisco, CA 94105
(415) 243-8003

Local Government Coordination
   Program
Box 583
Bodega Bay, CA 94923
(707) 875-3482

Natural Resources Defense Council
90 New Montgomery Street
San Francisco, CA 94105
(415) 777-0220

Natural Resources Defense Council
617 South Olive Street
Los Angeles, CA 90014
(213) 892-1500

Ocean Sanctuary Coordinating
   Committee
Box 498
Mendocino, CA 95460
(707) 937-0700

Western Oil and Gas Association
505 North Brand Boulevard
Suite 1400
Glendale, CA 91203
(818) 545-4105

DISTRICT OF COLUMBIA
American Oceans Campaign
235 Pennsylvania Avenue, S.E.
Washington, DC 20004
(202) 544-3526

Greenpeace
1436 U Street, N.W.
Washington, DC 20009
(202) 462-1177

Natural Resources Defense Council
1350 New York Avenue, N.W.
Washington, DC 20005
(202) 783-7800

FLORIDA
Florida Public Interest Research
   Group
308 East Park Avenue, Suite 213
Tallahassee, FL 32301
(904) 224-5304

Hoover Environmental Group
7420 S.W. 59th Avenue
Miami, FL 33143
(305) 665-6369

HAWAII
Natural Resources Defense Council
212 Merchant Street, Suite 203
Honolulu, HI 96813
(808) 533-1075

LOUISIANA
National Coalition for Marine
  Conservation
5113 Bissonet Drive
Metairie, LA 70003
(504) 455-2887

MASSACHUSETTS
Conservation Law Foundation
3 Joy Street
Boston, MA 02108
(617) 742-2540

NEW JERSEY
Clean Ocean Action
Box 505
Sandy Hook Highlands, NJ 07732
(201) 872-0111

NEW YORK
Group for the South Fork
Box 569
Bridgehampton, NY 11932
(516) 527-1400

Natural Resources Defense Council
  Coastal Project
40 West 20th Street
New York, NY 10011
(212) 727-2700

NORTH CAROLINA
Sierra Club
P.O. Box 272
Cedar Mountain, NC 28718
(704) 885-8229

Legasea
P.O. Box 460
Wanchese, NC 27981
(919) 441-2006

OREGON
Oregon Natural Resources Council
3921 S.E. Salmon
Portland, OR 97212
(503) 236-6528

TEXAS
Sierra Club
629 Euclid
Houston, TX 77009
(713) 640-4200

WASHINGTON
Friends of the Earth
4512 University Way, N.E.
Seattle, WA 98105
(206) 633-1661

Greenpeace
4649 Sunnyside Avenue North
Seattle, WA 98103
(206) 632-4326

Glossary

Affected state. A state that is or may be affected by activities on the outer continental shelf (OCS). The state(s) identified by the Secretary of the Interior for consultation on OCS leasing.

American Petroleum Institute (API). The trade association for the petroleum industry.

Area adjacent to a state. All of that portion of the OCS that is included within a planning area if such planning area is bordered by that state or is deemed by 30 CFR 252.2 to be adjacent to that state.

Area of hydrocarbon potential. An area that has the primary geologic characteristics favorable for the generation and the accumulation of hydrocarbons.

Associated gas. Free natural gas in immediate contact, but not in solution, with crude oil in the reservoir.

Barrel (BBL). A barrel of oil equals 42 gallons. The measure stems from the nineteenth century, when oil was carried in wooden fifty-gallon barrels that leaked an average of eight gallons during shipment and storage.

Bid. An offer for an OCS lease submitted by a potential lessee in the form of a cash bonus dollar amount or other commitments as specified in the final notice of sale.

Block. A geographical area having a square dimension of approximately three miles on a side, or nine square miles. It is used in official MMS leasing maps. See Tract.

Blowout. An uncontrolled flow of gas, oil, or other fluids from a well to the atmosphere. A well may blow out when formation pressure exceeds the pressure overburden of a column of drilling fluid.

Bonus. Money paid by the lessee for the execution of an oil and gas lease.

Coastal zone. Coastal waters and adjacent shoreland strongly influenced by each other.

Coastal zone consistency review. Review of federal licenses or permits and OCS plans pursuant to the Coastal Zone Management Act by affected coastal states to determine if the action is consistent with the state-approved CZM program.

Coastal Zone Management Act. A federal law enacted in 1972 to "protect, preserve, develop and, where possible, restore, or enhance the resources of the nation's coastal zone."

Cracking. A process carried out in a refinery reactor in which the large molecules in the crude stock are broken up into smaller, lower-boiling, stable hydrocarbon molecules, which leave the vessel as unfinished cracked gasoline, kerosene, and gas oil.

Crude oil. A mixture of liquid hydrocarbons that exists in natural underground reservoirs and remains liquid at atmospheric pressure after passing through surface separating facilities.

Development. Activities following exploration for, and discovery of, oil and gas, including the installation of facilities and the drilling and completion of wells for production purposes.

Development and production plan. A plan submitted by the oil company or developer to the MMS for approval that describes activities beyond exploration until the lease expires. The activities include facility installation, drilling, and production.

Drill cuttings. Chips and small fragments of rock that result from drilling and that are brought to the surface by the flow of the drilling mud as it is circulated.

Drill muds. A special mixture of clay, water or refined oil, and chemical additives pumped downhole through the drill pipe and drill bit to cool the bit, carry rock cuttings to the surface, and plaster the well walls to prevent collapse.

Drillship. A self-propelled, self-contained vessel equipped with a derrick for drilling wells in deep water.

Endangered species. A species of wildlife that is in immediate jeopardy of extinction from one or more causes, including loss or change of habitat, exploitation, predation, competition, disease, or other factors.

Environmental Assessment (EA). A concise public document required by the National Environmental Policy Act (NEPA). In the EA, a federal agency proposing an action provides evidence and analysis for determining whether it must prepare an Environmental Impact Statement or whether it finds there is no significant impact.

Environmental Impact Statement (EIS). A statement prepared by a federal agency to comply with NEPA for any major action that could have a significant effect on the environment.

Exclusive Economic Zone (EEZ). A geographic zone surrounding all U.S. territory extending from the seaward boundary of the territorial sea out to two hundred nautical miles from the shore.

Exploration. The process of searching for minerals prior to development. Activities include surveys, drilling, and delineation.

Exploration plan. A plan submitted by a lessee that identifies all the potential hydrocarbon accumulations and wells that the lessee proposes to drill to evaluate the accumulations within the lease or unit area covered by the plan.

Field. An area within which hydrocarbons have been concentrated and trapped in economically producible quantities in one or more structurally or stratigraphically related reservoirs.

Five-year program. A leasing program that consists of a schedule of proposed lease sales indicating the size, timing, and location of leasing activity that the Secretary of the Interior determines will best meet national energy needs for the five-year period following its approval.

Formation water. The water portion of the crude oil mixture that comes from the ground. It is contaminated with hydrocarbons and sometimes with heavy metals and hydrogen sulfide.

Gas. A light hydrocarbon gas mixture consisting chiefly of methane.

Geologic hazard. A feature or condition in the earth's geologic structure that may pose risks to oil exploration, development, or production activities.

Geophysics. The study of the earth's surface as revealed by differences in rock density and distribution; studied by means of seismic, magnetic, and gravity surveys.

Heavy metals. Certain potentially toxic metals such as barium, cadmium, chromium, copper, lead, mercury, nickel, silver, and zinc, often associated with drilling.

Hydrocarbon. Any of a large class of organic compounds containing primarily carbon and hydrogen. Hydrocarbons include crude oil and natural gas.

Hydrogen sulfide. A colorless, transparent gas with a characteristic rotten-egg smell. Short-term exposure to it can be lethal.

Jacket. A supporting structure for an offshore platform consisting of large-diameter pipe welded together with pipe braces to form a multilegged stoollike structure. The jacket is secured to the ocean floor by pilings driven through the legs.

Jack-up Rig. A mobile offshore drilling platform with extendable legs for support on the ocean floor.

Lease. A contract authorizing exploration for and development and production of minerals for a specified land area.

Lease sale. The process by which the MMS offers specific OCS tracts for lease. It includes leasing by competitive sealed bids.

Lease term. Duration of a lease. Oil and gas leases are issued for an initial period of five years to ten years. Once production occurs, the term continues as long as development occurs.

Marine sanctuary. An area protected under the federal Marine Protection Research and Sanctuaries Act of 1972.

Marine terminal. A facility that can receive or ship out crude oil or petroleum products on vessels.

Minimum royalty. The lowest payment a lessee must pay on a federal lease after production begins. Equivalent to the yearly rental, it is typically three dollars per acre or eight dollars per hectare offshore.

National Pollution Discharge Elimination System (NPDES). A system implemented by the EPA that regulates discharges into ocean waters.

Natural gas. A mixture of hydrocarbon compounds and small quantities of various nonhydrocarbons existing in gaseous phase at the surface or in solution with crude oil in natural underground reservoirs.

Offshore. That geographic area that lies seaward of the coastline.

Offshore storage and treatment vessel (OS&T). A converted tanker anchored near a platform that is used to remove natural gas, water, and other impurities from crude oil and to store the treated product until it is offloaded for transport to a refinery by a shuttle tanker.

Oil. A fluid composed of hydrocarbons.

Oil spill contingency plan. A plan submitted by the lessee to the MMS that details provisions for the fully defined, specific actions to be taken following discovery of an oil spill.

Outer continental shelf (OCS). The part of the continental shelf beyond the state-controlled three-mile limit.

Outer Continental Shelf Lands Act (OCSLA). A federal law enacted in 1953 that gave the Secretary of the Interior authority to grant mineral leases on submerged lands beyond the three-mile limit of the territorial sea to control development activities. The act was amended in 1978 to require the Secretary of the Interior to select the size, timing, and location of lease sales in a manner that balances the potential for oil discovery and the potential for environmental damage to the coastal zone.

Ozone. A major component of photochemical smog.

Pay. The subsurface geological formation in which a deposit of oil or gas is found in commercial quantities.

Petroleum. An oily, flammable, bituminous liquid that occurs in many places in the upper strata of the earth; most often a complex mixture of hydrocarbons of different types, with small amounts of other substances.

Planning area. Offshore geographical area designated by the MMS for potential lease sale offerings.

Platform. An offshore structure from which offshore wells are drilled, produced, or both. It consists of a jacket or welded frame that is positioned almost totally underwater and attached to the ocean floor with piles driven through hollow legs. The deck section where drilling activities occur is welded to the top of the jacket.

Production. The phase of oil and gas operations involved with well fluids extraction, separation, treatment, storage, measurement, and transportation.

Refinery. A plant for heating crude oil so that it separates into chemical components that are then distilled into more usable substances such as gasoline, kerosene, fuel oil, propane, and lubricants.

Reserves. A discovered resource. That portion of an identified oil or gas resource which can be economically extracted using current technology.

Reservoir. A subsurface, porous, permeable rock body in which oil, gas, or both have accumulated.

Rig. Equipment used for drilling an oil or gas well.

Royalty. A share of the minerals produced from a lease; a percentage of production either in money or in kind that a lessee is required to pay to the federal government.

Sale area. The grouping of whole and partial blocks within a specific planning area offered for sale.

Seismic. Pertaining to, characteristic of, or produced by earthquakes or earth vibrations; having to do with elastic waves in the earth.

Semisubmersible drill rig. A floating offshore drilling structure that has hulls submerged in the water but not resting on the seafloor.

Sour crude. Crude oil containing hydrogen sulfide, sulfur dioxide, carbon dioxide, or other acidic impurities.

Sour gas. Natural gas containing impurities, primarily hydrogen sulfide.

Stripper well. An onshore well that produces on average 2.71 barrels of oil per day.

Supply boat. Vessel that ferries people, food, water, and drilling equipment to a platform and returns to land with refuse that cannot be disposed of at sea.

Sweet gas. Gas that contains no hydrogen sulfide.

Tidelands. The portion of the continental shelf between the shore and the boundary marking state ownership.

Tract. A designation assigned for administrative and statutory purposes to a block or combination of blocks that are identified on a leasing map or an official protraction diagram prepared by the MMS. A tract may not exceed 5,760 acres unless it is determined that a larger area is necessary to comprise a reasonable economic production unit.

Trap. A geologic feature that permits the accumulation and prevents the escape of hydrocarbons from a reservoir.

Unit. A formally agreed-to consolidation by all lease interest owners whereby one operator explores, develops, and/or produces the leaseholdings for purposes of conservation, elimination of duplicate operations, and maximization of hydrocarbon recovery.

Viscosity. A measure of how easily a liquid will pour or flow.

Well. A hole drilled in the earth for the purpose of finding or producing crude oil or natural gas.

References

American Petroleum Institute. "California Offshore Energy: Promise and Challenge." September 1986.

Associated Press. "Exxon Cleanup Cost Put at $1.9 Billion," *San Francisco Chronicle*. December 5, 1989.

Baird, B. E. "California's Oil Spill Response Capability: Is it Adequate?" *Coastal Zone '83 Proceedings*. 1983.

Bleviss, Deborah. *Preparing for the 1990s: The World Automotive Industry and Prospects for Future Fuel Economy Innovation in Light Vehicles*. Federation of American Scientists, 1988.

Browne, Malcolm. "Noise Is Called a Threat to Sea Life," *New York Times*. December 13, 1988.

California Air Resources Board. "The Effects of Oxides of Nitrogen on California Air Quality." March 1986.

California Coastal Commission. Adopted Commission Findings on Consistency Certification, EPA's Draft NPDES general permits for discharges from offshore oil and gas facilities in federal waters off Southern California. February 1985.

California Department of Commerce. *The Economic Impact of Travel in California*. 1985.

California Energy Commission. "Conservation Report, October 1988."

"California's Risk in New Ocean Drilling," *San Francisco Chronicle*. May 24, 1989.

Canadian Petroleum Association. *Assessment of the Terrestrial Disposal of Waste Drilling Muds in Alberta: Chemistry of Sump Fluids and Effects on Vegetation and Soils*. December 1980.

Cavanagh, Ralph, *et al*. "Toward a National Energy Policy," *World Policy Journal*. Spring 1989.

Central Coast Regional Studies Program. Comments on the Draft Environmental Impact Statement OCS Lease Sale 91, Northern California of the Technical Review Panel. February 1988.

Congressional Research Service. *Renewable Energy: Federal Program and Congressional Interest*, Tables 2 and 3. March 2, 1988.

Department of the Interior, Minerals Management Service. *Draft Environmental Impact Statement* for Proposed Outer Continental Shelf Lease Sale 97, Beaufort Sea. 1987.

___ . *Draft Environmental Impact Statement* for Proposed Outer Continental Shelf Lease Sale 91, Northern California. Vol. 1. 1987.

____ . *Draft Environmental Impact Statement* for Proposed Outer Continental Shelf Lease Sale 116, Florida. 1987.

____ . *Estimates of Undiscovered Oil and Gas Resources in the United States—A Part of the Nation's Energy Endowment.* 1989.

____ . *Federal Offshore Statistics: 1988.*

____ . *Final Environmental Impact Statement* for Proposed Five-Year Outer Continental Shelf Leasing Program, Mid-1987-Mid-1992.

____ . *Final Environmental Impact Statement* for Proposed Outer Contintental Shelf Lease Sale 111, Mid-Atlantic. 1985.

____ . *Five-Year Outer Continental Shelf Oil and Gas Leasing Program Mid-1987 to Mid-1992: Proposed Final.* April 1987.

____ . *Leasing Energy Resources on the Outer Continental Shelf.* July 31, 1987.

____ . Materials dated April 7, 1986, and provided to Congressional Negotiating Team addressing leasing off the California coast.

____ . *Oil Spills, 1976-1985: Statistical Report.* 1986.

____ . *Prediction of Drilling Site Specific Interaction of Industrial Acoustic Stimuli and Endangered Whales in the Alaskan Beaufort Sea.* November 1987.

Egan, Timothy. "Pacific Oil Spill Renews Fear of Offshore Drilling," *New York Times.* January 8, 1989.

ERC Environmental and Energy Services Co., Inc. *Offshore Oil Development: Issues and Impacts for the Central California Coast.* May 1989.

Environmental Protection Agency. *Assessment of Environmental Fate and Effects from Offshore Oil and Gas Operations.* 1985.

____ . *Waste from the Exploration, Development, and Production of Crude Oil, Natural Gas and Geothermal Energy.* April 30, 1987.

Fish and Wildlife Service. *Comments on the Gulf of Mexico General NPDES Permit.* October 9, 1985.

____ . Letter to Regional Administrator of EPA Region VI regarding Draft General NPDES Permit for Oil and Gas Operations in the Gulf of Mexico. October 9, 1985.

"400,000-Gallon Oil Spill Off Huntington Beach," *San Francisco Chronicle.* February 8, 1990.

Geller, Howard. *Energy and Economic Savings Potential from National Appliance Efficiency Standards.* American Council on an Energy Efficient Economy. 1986.

____ . Testimony for House Appropriations Committee, Subcommittee on Transportation, on Appropriations for the Urban Mass Transit Administration, May 2, 1985.

Government Accounting Office. *Energy R&D: Changes in Federal Funding Criteria and Industry Response.* GAO/RCED-87-26. February 1987.

Grader, Zeke. Pacific Coast Federation of Fishermen's Associations. "Fisheries—Offshore Oil Conflicts," presented at Marin Environmental Forum. October 1987.

Graham, Frank. "Oil in the Sea: How Little We Know," *Audubon*. November 1978.

Griffiths, Robert P., *et. al*. "Long-Term Effects of Crude Oil on Uptake and Respiration of Glucose and Glutamate in Arctic and Subarctic Marine Sediments," in *Applied and Environmental Microbiology*. November 1981.

Gundlach, Eric, *et al*. "The Fate of Amoco Cadiz Oil," *Science*. July 8, 1983.

Herz, Michael J., and Dianne Kopec. *Analysis of the Puerto Rican Tanker Incident: Recommendations for Future Oil Spill Response Capability*. Paul F. Romberg Tiburon Center for Environmental Studies. October 31, 1985.

Hirst, Eric, and R. Goeltz. "Potential Versus Practice Installation of Retrofit Measures in the Hood River Conservation Project," Oak Ridge National Laboratory. ORNL/CON-189. 1985.

Howarth, Robert. "Oil and Fish: Can They Coexist?" in *Coast Alert, Scientists Speak Out*. 1981.

Hyland, Jeffrey L., *et al*. "Petroleum Hydrocarbons and Their Effects on Marine Organisms, Populations, Communities, and Ecosystems," in *Sources, Effects & Sinks of Hydrocarbons in the Aquatic Environment*. August 9, 1976.

Lancaster, John. "Crews Battle Oil Spills From 3 Tanker Accidents," *Washington Post*. June 25, 1989.

"Memories of 1969 Spill Still Linger Along Santa Barbara Coast," *San Francisco Examiner*. April 4, 1988.

Meyer Resources. *Offshore Oil Development: Economic Values of the Central California Coast*. 1986.

Mintz, Bill. "DOE: U.S. Could Lose Oil in Abandoned Fields," *Houston Chronicle*. February 1, 1990.

Mobil Oil. Editorial advertisement, *The Washington Post*. November 11, 1989.

Naj, Amal Kumar. "New Riches May Flow from Old Oil Wells," *Wall Street Journal*. February 2, 1990.

National Academy of Sciences. *Drilling Discharges in the Marine Environment*. 1983.

National Research Council. *The Adequacy of Environmental Information for Outer Continental Shelf Oil and Gas Decisions: Florida and California*. November 1989.

National Stripper Well Association. *National Stripper Well Survey*. A Joint Project of the Interstate Oil Compact Commission and the National Stripper Well Association. January 1988.

Natural Resources Defense Council. *The Auctioning of America's Coast*. 1987.

____. *Choosing an Electric Energy Future for the Pacific Northwest: An Alternative Scenario*. Department of Energy, Washington, D.C. 1980.

____. "Comments of the Natural Resources Defense Council on the Call for Information and Notice of Intent to Prepare an Environmental Impact Statement for OCS Lease Sale 108 in the South Atlantic." October 14, 1988.

____. "Comments of Natural Resources Defense Council on NHTSA Proposal to Reduce Passenger Car Corporate Average Fuel Efficiency Standards for Model Years 1989 and 1990." September 14, 1988.

____. "Comments of the Central Coast OCS Regional Studies Program and the Natural Resources Defense Council to the President's Outer Continental Shelf Leasing and Development Task Force." July 25, 1989.

____. *Energy Facts and Figures*. The Ocean Protection Act of 1990.

____. *Fact Sheet: Exxon Valdez Oil Spill*. September 12, 1989.

____. Testimony of Dr. David B. Goldstein Before the President's Outer Continental Shelf Leasing and Development Task Force, Santa Barbara, California, July 10, 1989.

____. Testimony of Lisa Speer before the Subcommittee on Interior and Related Agencies of the Committee on Appropriations, U.S. House of Representatives, on the Department of Interior's Offshore Oil and Gas Leasing Program (1987-1992). February 4, 1987.

____. Watson, Robert. "Fact Sheet on Oil and Conservation Resources." September 1988.

1986 Northwest Conservation and Electric Power Plan. Northwest Power Planning Council, 1986.

"Oil Pollution Lingers Longer," *New Scientist*. May 21, 1987.

Ott, Frederica. "Spilled Oil and the Alaska Fishing Industry," paper for 1989 Coastal-Open Water Oil Spill Conference. 1989.

Outer Continental Shelf Lands Act of 1953, as amended, 43 U.S.C. §§ 1344, 1345.

Palmer, Andrew, Ocean Policy Associates. "Offshore Oil From a DC Conservationist's Perspective: More Words from the Wise," *Wild Oregon: The Journal of the Oregon Natural Resources Council*. Winter 1987.

Rosenfeld, Arthur H., and David Hafemeister. "Energy-Efficient Buildings," *Scientific American*. April 1988.

Rotterman, L., and T. Simon-Jackson. "Sea Otter, *Enhydra Lutris*," in J. Lentfer, ed., Selected Marine Mammals of Alaska. 1988.

Sanders, Howard, et al. "Anatomy of an Oil Spill: Long-Term Effects from the Grounding of the Barge *Florida* off West Falmouth, Massachusetts," in *Journal of Marine Research*, Vol. 38, No. 2. 1980.

Shabecoff, Philip. "The Rash of Tanker Spills Is Part of a Pattern of Thousands a Year," *New York Times.* June 29, 1989.

"Skinner Defends Exxon Plan for a Halt in Alaska Cleanup," *New York Times.* July 26, 1989.

Spectra Information and Communication. *Understanding the Offshore Oil and Gas Development Process: A Citizen's Guide.* 1986.

Strosher, M. T., W. E. Younkin, and D.L. Johnson. "Assessment of Environmental Fate and Effects from Offshore Oil and Gas Operations." *Environment Reporter,* February 3, 1989.

"Tanker Hits Reef Off Oahu—117,000 Gallons of Oil Spilled," *San Francisco Chronicle.* March 4, 1989.

"The Lessons of Alaska: Major Spills and Close Calls of Recent History," *The Santa Rosa Press Democrat.* May 21, 1989.

Thomas, Paulette. "EPA Predicts Global Impact from Warming," *Wall Street Journal.* October 21, 1988.

Townsend, Richard, *et al. The Exxon Valdez Oil Spill: A Management Analysis.* September 1989.

Wald, Matthew. "Finding Oil in Doors and Lights," *The New York Times.* May 16, 1988.

Washington Sea Grant Program. *Information Priorities: Final Report of the Advisory Committee Ocean Resources Assessments Program.* 1988.

Wilson, T. "City Jailers Keeping Busy," *Valdez Vanguard.* September 6, 1989.

____ . "City Waste Facilities Getting Overwhelmed," *Valdez Vanguard.* August 30, 1989.

____ . "Cops Catching More Robbers," *Valdez Vanguard.* May 17, 1989.

____ . "Tourism Industry Here Is Suffering," *Valdez Vanguard.* August 9, 1989.

Index

ABOUT THE AUTHORS

DWIGHT HOLING is the author of *California Wild Lands: A Guide to The Nature Conservancy Preserves* and *Coral Reefs: Fragile Cities Beneath the Sea.* He has written articles on the environment for numerous publications, including *Discover, Omni, Audubon, Sierra, National Wildlife, Greenpeace,* and *The Amicus Journal.* He lives in Oakland, California, with his wife, Ann, and two children, Mary and Sam.

RICHARD CHARTER, author of Chapter Four, has served for the past nine years as Director of the California OCS Local Government Coordination Program. He coordinates the responses of cities and counties along the California coast to federal OCS leasing plans.

ALSO AVAILABLE FROM ISLAND PRESS

Ancient Forests of the Pacific Northwest
By Elliott A. Norse

Better Trout Habitat: A Guide to Stream Restoration and Management
By Christopher J. Hunter

The Challenge of Global Warming
Edited by Dean Edwin Abrahamson

The Complete Guide to Environmental Careers
The CEIP Fund

Creating Successful Communities: A Guidebook for Growth Management Strategies
By Michael A. Mantell, Stephen F. Harper, and Luther Propst

Crossroads: Environmental Priorities for the Future
Edited by Peter Borrelli

Economics of Protected Areas
By John A. Dixon and Paul B. Sherman

Environmental Restoration: Science and Strategies for Restoring the Earth
Edited by John J. Berger

Fighting Toxics: A Manual for Protecting Your Family, Community, and Workplace
Edited by Gary Cohen and John O'Connor

The Forest and the Trees: A Guide to Excellent Forestry
By Gordon Robinson

Forests and Forestry in China: Changing Patterns of Resource Development
By S. D. Richardson

Hazardous Waste from Small Quantity Generators
By Seymour I. Schwartz and Wendy B. Pratt

In Praise of Nature
Edited and with essays by Stephanie Mills

Natural Resources for the 21st Century
Edited by R. Neil Sampson and Dwight Hair

Overtapped Oasis: Reform or Revolution for Western Water
By Marc Reisner and Sarah Bates

Permaculture: A Practical Guide for a Sustainable Future
By Bill Mollison

The Poisoned Well: New Strategies for Groundwater Protection
Edited by Eric Jorgensen

Race to Save the Tropics: Ecology and Economics for a Sustainable Future
Edited by Robert Goodland

Recycling and Incineration: Evaluating the Choices
By Richard A. Denison and John Ruston

Research Priorities for Conservation Biology
Edited by Michael E. Soule and Kathryn Kohm

Resolving Environmental Disputes: Community Involvement in Conflict Resolution
By James E. Crowfoot and Julia M. Wondolleck

Rivers at Risk: The Concerned Citizen's Guide to Hydropower
By John D. Echeverria, Pope Barrow, and Richard Roos-Collins

Saving the Tropical Forests
By Judith Gradwohl and Russell Greenberg

Shading Our Cities: A Resource Guide for Urban and Community Forests
Edited by Gary Moll and Sara Ebenreck

War on Waste: Can America Win Its Battle With Garbage?
By Louis Blumberg and Robert Gottlieb

Wetland Creation and Restoration: The Status of the Science
Edited by Mary E. Kentula and Jon A. Kusler

Wildlife and Habitats in Managed Landscapes
Edited by Jon E. Rodiek

Wildlife of the Florida Keys: A Natural History
By James D. Lazell, Jr.

For a complete catalog of Island Press publications, please write:
Island Press
Box 7
Covelo, CA 95428
or call: 1-800-828-1302